Cage and Aviary Bird
Survival Manual

Cage and Aviary Bird
Survival Manual

A comprehensive family-by-family guide
to keeping cage and aviary birds

Graham Wellstead

BARRON'S

A QUARTO BOOK

Copyright © Quarto Inc.

First U.S. edition published in 1997 by
Barron's Educational Series, Inc.

All inquiries should be addressed to:
Barron's Educational Series, Inc.
250 Wireless Boulevard
Hauppauge NY 11788

Library of Congress Cataloging-in-Publication Data
Wellstead, Graham.
  Cage and aviary bird survival manual : a
comprehensive family-by-family guide to
keeping cage and aviary birds / Graham
Wellstead. – 1st U.S. ed.
    p.   cm.
  "A Quarto book"–T.p. verso.
  Includes index.
  ISBN 0-8120-9799-8
  1. Cage birds.   2. Aviculture.   I. Title.
SF461.W45   1997
636.6–dc21   97-7745
                                       CIP

This book was designed and produced by
Quarto Publishing plc
The Old Brewery
6 Blundell Street
London N7 9BH

Senior editor Michelle Pickering
Senior art editor Antonio Toma
Copy editor Ralph Hancock
Designer Peter Laws
Illustrator Lawrie Taylor
Photographers Colin Bowling, Paul Forrester
Picture research Giulia Hetherington,
Miriam Hyman
Editorial director Pippa Rubenstein
Art director Moira Clinch

Typeset by
Central Southern Typesetters, Eastbourne, UK
Manufactured by
Eray Scan Pte Ltd, Singapore
Printed by
Leefung-Asco Printers Ltd, China

ontents

Introduction 6

How to Use this Book 7

An Introduction to Keeping Cage and Aviary Birds

Cages, Bird Rooms, and Aviaries 8

Feeding 14

Breeding 16

Directory of Birds and their Care

Ducks and Geese 20

Birds of Prey 28

Pigeons and Doves 40

Pheasants and Quail 46

Parrots 56

Small Softbills 90

Small Seed Eaters 110

Starlings and Larger Softbills 138

Dealing with Disease 148

Glossary 152

Index 156

Credits 160

Introduction

My own introduction to keeping birds began when I helped my father feed and clean his large collection of budgerigars that he kept, not as a great exhibition breeding group, but as a way of supplementing a starvation wage working for a community of Anglican nuns. The sale of baby budgerigars helped keep the wolf from the door, but when the rising price of seed wiped out his profits, he sold them all. The end of his collection was the beginning of mine, for I was given a free hand with a large bird room and a set of connecting aviaries. Thus started a lifetime interest, interrupted for only a few years while I served with the army in Germany. As a single man, I lived in barracks and could not keep birds, but I bred Roller Canaries in a married friend's quarters.

The keeping of birds often becomes an obsession. Many keepers become animal behaviorists, and very good ones, too, learning by observation. Bird keeping is very much a "hands on" operation, with aviculturalists becoming very close to their birds, far more so than most ornithologists. As a result, much scientific knowledge, and many projects aimed at saving species from certain extinction, have been founded on avicultural experience. This is certainly the case with many of the endangered parrot projects and all those for birds of prey.

If you intend to keep birds, you must understand that they depend entirely on you. You decide what they eat, when they eat, whether they breed or not, when they breed, often which other birds they breed with, how they live, and even when they die. This power should never be taken lightly; birds are a full-time responsibility. As long as you maintain only single-species collections, such as parakeets or canaries, you may be able to leave them in the care of others while you take a vacation. If the collection expands into specialist areas, such as nectar feeders, you can almost never find qualified people to take over from you. In the past I have seen quite a number of aviculturalists with specialized collections of birds give up simply because a change of job or other circumstances kept them from caring for their birds as they should.

I would say you should never buy any living thing on impulse; but we are all human, and I am as guilty, probably more guilty, than most. Entering the premises of a large bird dealer, or a private collection, I find myself behaving like a kid turned loose in a candy store. However, as I get older, I seem to be behaving more sensibly, at least some of the time. Therefore, at the risk of being called a hypocrite, I would urge self-restraint.

Bird keeping should be a relaxing and pleasurable hobby. If you keep your birds in good condition, and do not overstep your budget or the time you can devote to them, your birds will give you nothing but pleasure.

Section One

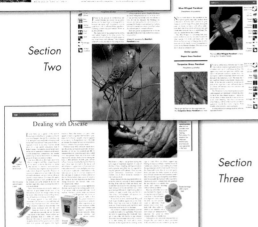

Section Two

Section Three

How to Use this Book

This book is divided into three easy-to-use sections, which together give comprehensive guidance to the novice aviculturalist. Section One is a general introduction to the hobby, including basic information that beginners should know – how to set up a cage, bird room, or aviary; the many types of bird food that particular species may require; and advice on breeding.

Section Two is a detailed directory of birds, subdivided into bird families. The entry for each bird includes a photograph and a description of its physical characteristics, together with advice on the care of that species. Each bird is also key-coded with simple symbols that are easily understood without any need to cross-check (see right for a detailed explanation). Wherever appropriate, a list of related birds that require the same type of care is given under the heading "Similar species." The Directory of Birds features those birds most commonly seen in aviculture as well as a wide choice of the more rare but avidly sought species.

Section Three deals with the potential problem of disease and explains how to recognize and treat many common diseases. It also contains a comprehensive glossary of terms commonly used by aviculturalists.

A Guide to the Key Symbols

Indicates the level of care and experience required to keep a bird, on a scale of 1 to 10, with 1 being those birds particularly suitable for beginners.

Gives size of bird from tip of beak to tip of tail. Use this as an initial guide to determining the size of environment required.

Indicates those birds for which a cage is the most suitable environment.

Indicates those birds for which a bare aviary is the most suitable environment.

Indicates those birds for which a planted aviary is the most suitable environment.

Shows whether additional heating is essential, required some of the time, or is unnecessary.

Gives details of whether particular birds should be kept alone or as a pair, in a single-species colony, if a bird is likely to attack smaller companions, or if it will mix well with any other birds.

Shows if a bird is very noisy, noisy at times, or quiet.

Indicates how many eggs a bird will typically produce in a single clutch.

States how many days of incubation are required before hatching.

Cages, Bird Rooms, and Aviaries

Light, fresh air, and exercise keep your birds in good condition, something difficult to achieve without an **aviary**.

The environment you provide for your birds is very often the key to your success. Too often the keeper has to adapt and improvise. A cage designed to fit into a living room may be suitable for a single pet parakeet or canary, but entirely unsuitable for other species. Such glittering all-wire contraptions offer no security or protection from drafts or sunlight. If birds have to be kept in a cage, a box cage is almost always the best option.

In aviaries, destructive species such as large parrots, or nervous species such as most falcons, require special environments. There is little

point in giving a pair of parrots a wood-framed, planted aviary: the birds will destroy the plants in a few days and chew their way out of the wooden structure in a few weeks. Similarly, falcons kept in an all-wire aviary will smash themselves to pieces on the wire in days, and their droppings will kill any plants.

The size and design of cages and aviaries alike need to take the species into consideration. It may sound odd to say that an aviary can be too large, but for safety and security this is often the case, and many collections of birds open to the

public have their stock on display in aviaries larger than is really required simply to satisfy the demands of a public who do not understand the needs of the birds. Very often, it is the smaller off-exhibit aviaries where successful breeding takes place. In many countries, there is a legal minimum size for cages, which makes sense but is sometimes difficult to interpret. For example, a bird cage must be large enough for the occupant to spread its wings in any direction. This makes almost all parrot cages smaller than the law requires. The fact that many pet parrots spend more time out of their cage than in is no defense. It is against the law to restrict any bird for periods longer than one hour, except for traveling or at an exhibition. On the other hand, the minimum size allowed for a canary, $10 \times 8 \times 8$ inches ($25 \times 20 \times 20$ cm), is still too small in my view. A cage should allow any bird to keep its feathers in good order. Too many large macaws have their tail feathers shredded and broken because the cage is not adequate.

There are very few species of small birds that cannot be successfully kept in cages, and suitably sized box cages are the standard fitting for the bird rooms of most serious aviculturalists. Box cages are not just convenient; many species feel comfortable in this type of cage, and remain relaxed and in good condition. Box cages are just that, boxes with a wire front. They are available in a multitude of sizes and a number of materials. The most usual are plywood and melamine-faced blockboard. A more expensive option is stove-enameled steel. Plastic is becoming more popular, since it lasts well and is easily cleaned, which is very important, for it is essential that cages be kept clean and free of bacterial buildup. I have never understood how canaries are able to achieve the seemingly impossible feat of depositing their droppings on the ceiling of a cage.

If you decide to build your own cages, for example to fit your bird room, it is important to research the design properly. A standard treble

Bird rooms are necessary if you intend to keep a large collection of small birds.

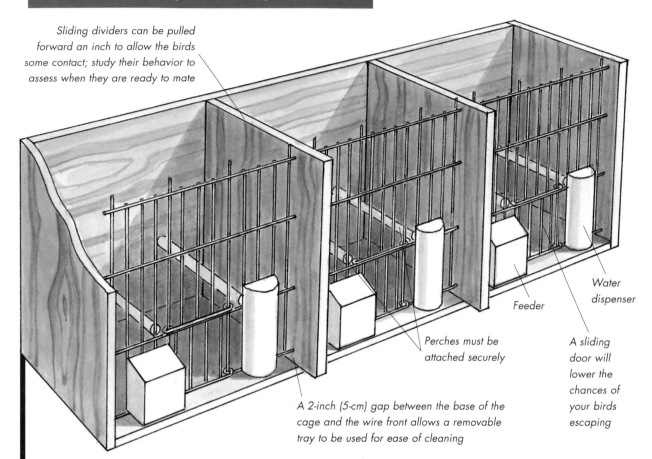

Sliding dividers can be pulled forward an inch to allow the birds some contact; study their behavior to assess when they are ready to mate

Water dispenser

Feeder

Perches must be attached securely

A sliding door will lower the chances of your birds escaping

A 2-inch (5-cm) gap between the base of the cage and the wire front allows a removable tray to be used for ease of cleaning

This **treble breeding cage** is suitable for canaries and small finches and will give them a feeling of security when nesting.

breeding cage for canaries and small finches is 42 inches long × 10 inches deep × 15 inches high (106 × 25 × 38 cm), divided in three by removable sliding panels. However, it is better to increase it to 48 × 14 × 16 inches (122 × 35 × 40 cm); the extra size will make little difference to the service space in a room, but gives much more space inside, and a feeling of greater security for nesting birds. A double breeding cage is also suitable but a treble allows you to put a male bird in the center section and a female on either side, thus improving the chances of compatibility.

When building a number of breeding cages, it is often best to build in block form, that is in one unit three or four cages high. The resulting saving on materials may allow you to improve the quality of the accommodations. It is important not to cut corners, but to build well and to last. The cage may be no more than a simple rectangular box, but the arrangement of the front and the floor will make a great difference for good or bad.

The design of the wire front needs some thought. What should the bar spacing be? Do you need feeder holes? Are the doors large enough to service the inside and allow nest pans or boxes to be taken in and out, while not large enough to allow the escape of tiny finches, which move like lightning? Cage front manufacturers provide a vast array of options from stock, but if your needs are not met, they will generally build fronts to your specifications at little extra cost. The front rails should allow the entire cage front to be removed for cleaning. Trying to scrub out a cage through a 5-inch (10-cm) door will soon illustrate the need for this. The bottom rail should allow space for a deep removable tray. Too often, the bottom rail is so close to the cage floor that stray seed and droppings jam the tray when you are trying to slide it out. I like a tray at least 2 inches (5 cm) deep, which allows easy removal and also retains most of the seed husks and other detritus that appear on the cage floor. All species of birds benefit from bathing and in doing so splash water everywhere. The resultant damage to wood or masonite tray bases makes the extra cost of steel or aluminum trays well worthwhile.

The interior of a cage may look attractive painted in gleaming white, but I have found many birds are much more at ease in pale green or blue, so much so that breeding improves significantly. Many bird keepers, including parrot keepers, now house their birds in all-wire suspended cages that keep maintenance and cleaning to a minimum. While I understand their feelings, and the breeding success rate shows the birds are reasonably happy, I do feel that the sterile environment leaves something to be desired. Most bird keepers start off with a converted garden shed, or a spare room in the house, as their first bird room. Many never advance beyond that stage, while others go on to build palatial constructions that surpass their own living conditions with computer-controlled environments, running water, and even piped music.

The minimum size for a bird room fitted with tiered breeding cages is 6 × 8 ft. (1.8 × 2.4 m). If a garden shed is used, it must be provided with good lighting and ventilation. These vital requirements for good health are inadequate in most small sheds. Temperature control is also important; a single-skinned wooden construction needs added insulation, or the bird room will be an oven on a hot day and a freezer on a cold one. If you are improving lighting by enlarging windows, you should also install safety screens. These avoid injury to birds hitting a closed window, and escape if the window is open. The door should also be secure and backed up by a safety door. It is amazing how many birds escape, either when the door is left open or, having escaped from their cage, through the door when the keeper opens it.

When using a small building as a bird room, it is worth considering using skylights rather than conventional windows. This leaves wall space free for additional cages or an inside flight. Natural lighting is always by far the best, but there are times when artificial lighting is a must. The choice of lighting now available includes fluorescent tubes that closely mimic daylight. Dimmers and preset timers now let you control day length with-

out the problem of forgetting to turn off the bird-room lights, as I have done in the past. With small exotic species, additional day length gives a longer time to feed, very important during long, dark winters in northern areas.

Heating is not always needed in a temperate climate. Species such as canaries, European finches, and parakeets do not really need a heated bird room, but exotic softbills and small seed eaters will not survive in temperate areas without some form of heating. Tubular electric heaters and fan heaters, which should be thermostatically controlled, are usually preferred. Be sure they are strong enough to keep the temperature at the required level during very cold weather.

Whatever type of facility you use, it should be easy to clean and verminproof. A buildup of discarded food attracts vermin, and mice, rats, and ants are easier to attract than to repel. Any wooden structure placed directly on the ground is a gift to vermin trying to get inside, so you should either have a solid concrete base or raise the structure above the ground. If you use a solid concrete base, do not forget to lay a waterproof membrane under the concrete, or any floor covering will quickly draw water through, filling the room with the smell of decay and mildew. My bird room is raised above the ground with a clear space underneath, so that I can see any signs of unwanted visitors before opening the door. Brick buildings are especially prone to dampness unless properly constructed and ventilated.

If you use rodenticides to kill mice or rats, take great care where you place the poisoned bait, which is usually made from grain. Keepers of birds of prey must be especially careful, for their birds will try to kill any rodents that enter their quarters, and if they have already taken

You may need to provide special **heating** arrangements for your birds. Tubular heaters are safe and reliable.

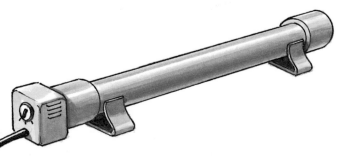

Honeysuckle produces rapid growth and promotes insects.

Clematis is an attractive cover plant for the summer months.

Laburnum is attractive but highly poisonous to humans and birds alike.

poison, they will be lethal to the birds. Technology has now come to our aid with the invention of sonic vermin repellents that emit high-frequency sound, above the upper limit of human hearing, to drive away rodents. If you live in an area where rodents abound, it would make sense to investigate the cost of such a unit.

There are as many kinds of aviary as there are of cages, if not more. Manufacturers can provide a choice to suit most pockets, from a small wire flight with an inside shelter to a vast structure designed to suit the largest species. If you decide to build your own, as with cages and bird rooms, build well and build to last. With planted aviaries, particularly those that have plants growing up the sides, the wire must be of the highest quality, for replacing it is an arduous task.

Whatever the size of your aviary, and even if it is only occupied during summer months, a proper shelter is a must. A small built-on shelter may be ignored by the birds unless it is light inside, and the food supply is placed there. It is generally simpler to cover one end and part of the roof.

Planting should be done with care, avoiding any plant that may be poisonous. Yew, laurel, and laburnum should not be in or near the aviary. Climbing plants add color as well as cover, but are probably best planted outside a small aviary, for it is important to retain as much flying space as possible. There are many attractive species of honeysuckle and clematis that make ideal plants for garden aviaries, with Russian vine as a standby for rapid establishment of cover, and also to provide a source of insect food. Note, though, that this rampant plant will take over the whole of a small aviary in one season unless it is ruthlessly cut back.

The aviary floor needs to be concrete if parrots are the occupants, but it can be gravel or grass for most other species. Concrete and gravel allow easy cleaning, with washed gravel giving an especially fresh look. If the aviary roof is covered, sand over a concrete base allows small finches, canaries, and parakeets to forage for grit. A dry floor is easier to maintain, and sand can be washed, dried, and reused. I make it a standard practice to underwire any aviary that does not have a concrete floor, and also bury a heavy-gauge close wire mesh around

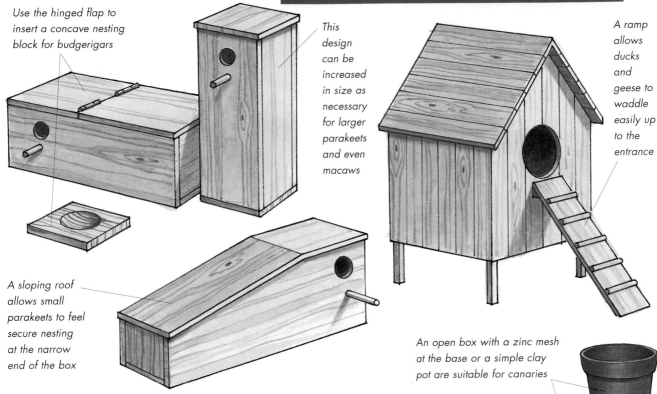

Use the hinged flap to insert a concave nesting block for budgerigars

This design can be increased in size as necessary for larger parakeets and even macaws

A ramp allows ducks and geese to waddle easily up to the entrance

A sloping roof allows small parakeets to feel secure nesting at the narrow end of the box

An open box with a zinc mesh at the base or a simple clay pot are suitable for canaries

A variety of **nesting boxes**, all of which provide a private and secure environment for breeding birds.

the perimeter at a minimum depth of 18 inches (45 cm). This keeps both rodents and foxes out, and keeps enthusiastic diggers such as pheasants in.

Very small aviaries should not have grass floors, for with all species the grass usually cannot stand the wear it is likely to get. On the other hand, a planted aviary of a good size can often become an extension of the backyard, and I have often seen aviaries in which lawns and flowerbeds flow naturally through the enclosure uninterrupted. If your aviary is large enough to support it, a shallow pond could be added as a feature; but there are dangers in ponds, especially with birds that bathe at inappropriate times, such as just before roosting. With ground-dwelling species, it is possible that night disturbance may cause them to fall into the water and drown.

Water is vital for waterfowl, however, and if these birds are kept in an aviary, the water supply needs to be constant and fresh. You should be aware of the dangers of digging a deep pond within an aviary. Initially such a pond will be welcomed, and your ducks will have a wonderful time diving and swimming in the clear water. But in a remarkably short time, the water will turn brown,

then black, and will soon be no better than an open sewer. Changing the water in a deep pond is a major exercise; it is far better to construct a shallow pond that can be quickly drained and cleaned. I am not in favor of letting the water drain out over the surrounding area and prefer any water flushed from a pond to go into the drains.

Waterfowl kept in a small yard may bring legal problems with local environmental officials unless strict attention is given to the method of cleaning. Indeed, any aviary should be built in accordance with local planning regulations. If you have close neighbors, it is sensible to advise them of any plans you have and also make them aware of the type of birds you intend to keep. In urban areas, the height of any construction may be controlled, as is the distance from the boundary fence. If you get the dimensions wrong, not only will you upset your neighbors, you may be forced to tear your aviary down in the middle of the breeding season.

The variety of options for housing birds of any species is enormous. Several specialist publications cover this subject alone, and give full details of construction. Get your aviary right the first time, and you will save yourself endless problems.

Feeding

We live in a time when foodstuffs that were previously seasonal are available all year round, and from all over the world. This applies not only to people, but also to birds. So there is no justification for cutting corners and penny pinching when feeding them. If the food you provide is not fresh enough for you to eat, it will not do for your birds either. It is madness to buy a bird for a large sum and then feed it substandard food in order to save money.

Seed suppliers today generally pride themselves on the quality of their products. Canary seed and millet should shine as though varnished. With certain exceptions, the best quality seeds have almost no smell. Anything that has a musty odor is not suitable for your birds, or wild birds either. Recent research has shown that poor conditions in many backyard feeding stations have reduced the numbers of garden birds rather than increased them.

Green food needs to be carefully gathered. Wild foods such as dandelion, chickweed, the seeding heads of evening primroses, teasels, thistles, and grasses must be collected from places that have not been polluted in any way. Much of your birds' green food requirements can be grown in your backyard, especially brassicas and legumes. It is simple to produce highly nutritious and safe green food from the special "soak seed" mixtures put together by most seed merchants. You can also grow various kinds of bean sprouts, as favored by vegetarians and Chinese food fans.

Fruits must be fresh, ripe, and perfect. Apples, pears, oranges, grapes, and tomatoes are available everywhere throughout the year; pomegranates and other exotic fruits less so. Berries of wild plants such as hawthorn, blackberries, honeysuckle berries, and rosehips may be picked fresh and then frozen for use at any time. Dried fruits such as raisins, apricots, and figs may be either soaked or fed as they come. I find many birds love dried figs, including canaries, which like them split in half to give themselves access to the soft inner fruit and the seeds, as well as parakeets and parrots. Take advantage of the late summer glut of foods such as corn on the cob; buy in bulk and freeze them. Large parrots are particularly fond of corncobs.

All seeds, grains, and pellet food should be stored safely away from vermin. Waterfowl and pheasants are notorious attractors of rats and mice, and improper storage is asking for trouble.

Food for birds of prey is generally bought frozen and defrosted as required. It is difficult to check the condition of ready-frozen day-old chick culls, rats, mice, or quail, and you must simply buy from a supplier you can trust. Do not take the easy option of picking up road kills as a free supply. Wild animals are either quick or dead when crossing a road. Experienced creatures learn to be quick. Therefore the slow ones are suspect and may already be dying from some affliction. Something which, on the face of it, appears to be a free meal for your stock may be a death sentence.

Most insectivores are fed on commercially prepared foods – balanced diets, carefully formulated for the species – but birds must learn to eat them before they can benefit. Many must have live food, and some will eat nothing else. A diet of mealworms alone is not a good one, and the birds must be weaned onto a better diet if they are to survive. Live foods – mealworms, buffalo worms, wax moth larvae, crickets, locusts, and fruit fly larvae – need to be given in quantity, added to the commercial mixture, which contains cereals, fruit, dried insects, honey, and animal fat. Grated cheese, chopped hardboiled eggs, and finely chopped raw meat such as heart may be added, together with a vitamin supplement and a probiotic powder to stimulate appetite. I do not like to use gentle, blowfly, or housefly larvae, which need to be cleaned in bran for several days

before they may be safely used. I do use the pupae and the adult flies, slowly released through a small hole in their container. Finally, the backyard and large trees can be a major source of a wide variety of live food. Use a cane or stick to shake the branches and an upturned umbrella to catch what falls out of them.

Good feeding produces good stock, for we are what we eat.

Fresh, good quality food is essential to keep birds healthy and content.

1 Fruit fly culture (in grass)
2 Canary rearing food
3 Worming capsules
4 Vitamin supplement
5 Dried insect mixture
6 Small softbill food
7 Cuttlefish bones
8 Canary mixture
9 Probiotic powder
10 Parrot mixture
11 Trace element supplement
12 Mealworms
13 Parakeet mixture

Breeding

Most bird breeders will tell you they started off with one bird, obtained another, bred a few, bought some more, bred a few more, and so on, their hobby expanding almost imperceptibly toward an eventual takeover of their lives.

Breeding birds adds interest to aviculture; the pleasure of seeing your birds produce eggs and chicks, which grow to maturity while attended by devoted parents. But we breeders are not just enjoying ourselves; we are also trying to establish our various species in adequate numbers to be fully self-sufficient. Over the past few years, many previously available wild birds have become unobtainable, and many more will also become so. Species that were common when I was a boy are now virtually unknown as captive birds. Even some domesticated species are now in such low numbers as to cause concern. It is important to keep the gene pool as large as possible, for once diversity is gone, it takes centuries or millennia to recover.

If you intend to breed your birds, you should give serious thought to how you are going to achieve success, and also to how you will house your expanded numbers. The bigger the size of the birds, the bigger the problem.

Improved management and greater knowledge of the requirements of species now mean that many species that were considered unlikely ever to breed are now being bred in considerable numbers. Parrots and birds of prey are notable examples. A very diverse collection may be interesting, but it is not always the best way to proceed. Specialization is the way forward, a fact that most zoological collections have accepted. For some species, this recent trend is too late; for others it is just in time. A number of collections have held individual birds for years on end, simply because the specimens were part of the collection. A Lear's Macaw, desperately rare, sat on a perch in a French zoo for 25 years before it was eventually united with a mate, similarly held in a British zoo. Now with a noted private keeper skilled in breeding rare parrots, the two birds may yet breed and increase the gene pool in time.

In such instances, pairing considerations are secondary, for there are few alternative mates. However, for many species there are stud books intended to keep the gene pool as open as possible, avoiding inbreeding. With the more common species, such as many of the small waxbills, colony breeding will allow birds to select their own mates, which makes for compatibility. This is often very important, especially in species where the sexes are hard to tell apart.

Until recently, it was quite usual to find two birds living in an aviary, assumed to be a pair, but that eventually turned out to be the same sex. There is no need for this situation to occur now, because birds, especially those of large or rare species, are often sexed by surgical methods or DNA analysis. Surgical sexing is expensive and dangerous, and can only be of value if the birds are either sexually mature or very close to it. However, DNA sexing is now available at affordable prices, and involves only a drop of

Breeding birds is an extremely satisfying experience. These Bullfinches and their brood have created a near natural environment.

blood or two freshly plucked feathers to give a result that may save years of fruitless waiting. A common problem is that many birds that show no dimorphism often exhibit behavior that leads the keeper to believe they are a true pair. Apparent mating and egg laying may occur when two hens are present, and mating without eggs when the two are both males. But even birds of opposite sexes may be incompatible and fight, or simply ignore each other. Here, a change of partners can produce dramatic results.

Even when your birds have laid eggs, your problems are far from over. The eggs may be fertile and all going well when suddenly the parents give up. Here you need to decide on fostering or artificial incubation. With small birds, incubation is often not an option and you must foster the eggs, or chicks, if they are to survive. With birds of prey, pheasants, and parrots, this has become almost the norm for many species. The value or rarity of the birds is too high to allow nature to take its course, although I should state at this stage – unless the species is very rare – that I refuse to interfere with any of my birds. Either they lay, brood, hatch, and rear eggs, or they don't.

There is a case for the artificial propagation of rare species, for which several methods may be employed. Where a species is really scarce, it makes sense to use the method known as egg pulling; that is, removing each egg as it is laid. This stimulates the birds to lay a much larger clutch than usual. Alternatively, and a method that is much preferred, the birds are double-clutched: eggs are not removed until the clutch is completed and incubation has already begun. This is a very popular method with hawk breeders, for the parent birds will produce a second clutch in 14 days. The chicks from the first clutch are hand-reared for between 5 and 12 days and then returned to their parents, who usually exhibit no surprise at the sudden appearance of well-grown chicks, and begin feeding them almost immediately.

This is not a recommended practice for parrots or pheasants, however. Most parrot breeders prefer to take either eggs by pulling or double-clutching for incubation, or small chicks, which are then hand-reared to be sold as tame pet birds.

The number of pet parrots produced is now quite astonishing, and I often wonder where they all go. There are problems with these methods of overproducing birds, not the least being that the parent birds may become very stressed by the constant removal of their eggs or chicks. I recently saw a pair of very productive African Gray parrots, the female of which had taken to feather plucking with a vengeance. Her owner appeared unaffected by this, and I had great difficulty not showing my anger and concern.

Hand-reared parrots, especially those reared in isolation, often exhibit behavioral problems when they reach sexual maturity. They are an accident waiting to happen in many cases, and a jealous parrot can inflict horrific injuries should it decide to do so. Additionally, many such birds are unable to breed naturally. They may be unaware of their own species – that is, they are malimprinted. Such a trend should not be encouraged. Other birds that suffer problems with breeding are the pheasant and quail species, particularly the small Chinese and Japanese Quail, which have mostly lost the instinct to incubate their own eggs.

In many instances, manipulation of a bird's breeding cycle has gone beyond the original aim of saving rare species and is now done purely for commercial gain. However, no responsible aviculturist would indulge in such a practice.

Artificial incubation is often the only answer to successful breeding.

Directory of Birds and their Care

Ducks and Geese 20

Birds of Prey 28

Pigeons and Doves 40

Pheasants and Quail 46

Parrots 56

Small Softbills 90

Small Seed Eaters 110

Starlings and Larger Softbills 138

Ducks and Geese

Like most people, I suspect, my first introduction to birds at close quarters was as a toddler feeding the ducks in the local park. There can be few people who do not enjoy feeding ducks, and the keeping of exotic waterfowl is almost certainly only restricted by their need for greater space and larger quantities of water than most other birds. Ducks have a charm and fascination all their own and, provided you have the space, are very easy to provide for. Most do very well on grain, pelleted food, and chopped greens of all kinds.

Before embarking on keeping ducks, you should look at the facilities offered by other duck keepers, especially in winter. Until you have witnessed the ruin ducks can wreak on a small area of suburban yard, you will find it difficult to believe. Ducks can not only be messy but noisy, and the results may go so far as to be actionable if neighbors object to the noise and smell. On the "Don't do as I do – Do as I say!" principle, I once dug a pond in a small yard, which I lined with plastic and happily filled with water, without first giving consideration to how I could keep the water clean. My ducks waited patiently for it to fill, and then, to my surprise and delight, dived in and swam underwater. One week later, three domestic ducks had turned my glittering pond into a stinking cesspool, which I had to empty by hand. One hundred and eighty 3-gallon buckets of dirty water poured into the sewer every Saturday morning soon took the edge off the pleasure of keeping ducks. Though it was only a small pond, after a short time it seemed unmanageably huge. I eventually came to my senses and gave up ducks in that yard, filled in the pond, and grew roses fed with wonderfully nutritious duck manure.

Most species of ducks and geese need clean water with access to grass – particularly geese, which are primarily grazers – and sheltered areas where they can preen and rest. Diving ducks need deep water. If you are unable to provide water for swimming, you must keep only those species that do not find water essential; but even so, make sure there is a supply of clean water in a receptacle deep enough for the ducks to immerse

A male
**Mandarin
Duck**
displaying its
spectacular
plumage.

their faces; otherwise, eye problems soon build up. Preferring to live in the open, ducks will rarely use a shed or shelter, so you do need to provide shrubs or trees as sun, rain, or wind breaks. Most species will live as part of a community, although some species need to be kept separate during the breeding season.

Although most species are quite free breeders, many keepers use artificial incubation and rearing techniques to improve their chances, especially with the more valuable or endangered species. If you are breeding exotic species in open accommodations, the birds need to be either wing clipped or pinioned. Wing clipping only works until the birds molt, when they may often replace feathers quicker than you expect and fly away. If

you consider pinioning as an option – that is, the removal of one wing tip at the wrist joint – then the duckling should be pinioned at a very early age, and under veterinary supervision. Adult birds may only be pinioned under a general anesthetic.

The general management of ducks must include protection from mammalian predators. Foxes, rats, mink, and even cats will return again and again once they discover the source of a free meal. In some areas, you must also protect against avian predators. Ducks generally need a quiet life, for many are very nervous and highly strung, and ducklings are particularly prone to stress, which may prove fatal. But if reared and maintained with care, ducks make interesting and charming additions to any collection.

The graceful **Canada Goose** requires a large expanse of water and plenty of grazing.

Ease of care (scale 1–10) 2

 22.5 in. (56 cm)

 Heating unnecessary

 Good mixer

 Noisy at times

 3–8 eggs

 25–28 days incubation

Red-Breasted Goose

(Branta ruficollis)

This small Siberian goose is a good subject for the keeper of exotic ducks and geese. It is colorful and becomes very tame and confiding; also it will almost certainly be considered a seriously endangered species in its natural habitat before long. Mainly black, this species has white wing bars and tail coverts, and bands of white that separate the chestnut breast from the black belly and ring the chestnut cheek patches. The beak and feet are also black.

Red-Breasted Geese are hardy. They mix well and are extremely decorative, a popular and very attractive species. A diet of pelleted foods alone is not acceptable. Wholemeal bread and some grain will be taken but a good area of grazing is essential, which may be supplemented with extra green food during winter months.

A **Red-Breasted Goose** showing off its striking markings in the sunlight.

Breeding is occasionally difficult to achieve, and because the species is valuable, it is most often propagated by artificial incubation rather than by letting nature take its course.

 Ease of care (scale 1–10) 1

 22–26 in. (55–65 cm)

 Heating unncessary

 May attack smaller birds

 Noisy at times

 5–10 eggs

 25–28 days incubation

Canada Goose

(Branta canadensis)

The large and attractive **Canada Goose** requires considerable space.

Found naturally in the northern United States and Canada, wintering in the south, this species has been introduced into many areas, including Britain, where it is now so numerous that it is regarded as a pest species. There are some ten subspecies, which vary in size and readiness to breed. If you have the water space for these large geese, in most areas they will arrive uninvited. The species is barred brown and gray above, with a black neck and a distinctive white patch on the cheeks and upper throat, and barred white below with a white rump and black tail. The sexes are alike.

Breeding geese split into pairs to defend territory, but when the goslings are established the parents generally associate with other pairs and raise their offspring in a nursery, sharing parental duties on a shift system.

Feed them a diet of grain and extra greens to supplement their grazing during the cold winter months.

Similar species

Barnacle Goose
Brent Goose

Mandarin Duck

(Aix galericulata)

This native of China, Japan, and northeastern Asia is an extremely ornamental species. The nuptial plumage of the drake is incredible: dark and glossy green above with dark brown wings, two chestnut feathers standing up on the back like small sails, iridescent maroon breast, glossy green forehead, and bronze-green crest.

The spectacular nuptial plumage of the male **Mandarin** far outshines that of the female.

The sides of the face and the crest are white, the flanks orange, and the bill red. The duck is streaked brown and gray, with a gray head and a white eye ring. In its eclipse plumage, the drake looks similar. Failure to pinion or wing clip the ducklings in the past has made this species well established as a feral bird in parts of Europe. The very similar Carolina Duck vies with the Mandarin as the most popular waterfowl species.

A diet of pelleted food, grain, and green food will be supplemented by foraging. It is a hole nester and requires a raised nest box or basket. When first hatched the ducklings are nervous and care should be taken not to stress them.

Similar species

Carolina Duck

Ease of care (scale 1–10)

18 in. (45 cm)

Heating unnecessary

May attack smaller birds

Quiet

8–12 eggs

29–30 days incubation

European Wigeon

(Anas penelope)

Ranging throughout Europe and Asia and migrating to winter in the Middle East, India, or Japan, depending on the starting point, this is a widespread species. The drake is gray above, finely vermiculated with black and white markings below, with black primary feathers and green speculum, a chestnut breast, head, and neck, and a buff forehead and crown. The duck is brown with pale underparts.

The European Wigeon has been kept as a captive species for a very long time, and is one of several believed to have been maintained in ancient Egypt. Although it will feed on grain and wholemeal bread with the usual chopped greens, this popular duck is a grazing bird and without good grass will not do well.

Very hardy and a good mixer, the Wigeon will breed well, and frequently hybridizes with other related species. A ground nester, it needs cover and will use a nest box.

The male **European Wigeon** has delicate gray markings and a distinctive copper head.

Similar species

Chloe Wigeon
American Wigeon
Green-Winged Teal

Ease of care (scale 1–10)

18 in. (45 cm)

Heating unnecessary

Good mixer

Noisy at times

7–10 eggs

25 days incubation

Ease of care (scale 1–10) 1

 22.5 in. (56 cm)

 Heating unnecessary

 Good mixer

 Quiet

 6–8 eggs

 26–28 days incubation

Laysan Teal

(Anus platyrhynchos laysanensis)

Dark brown with a buff margin to the feathers and a sooty brown head, a white ring around the eye, and a green speculum bordered in black and white, this is not the most colorful of ducks, but what it lacks in color it makes up in personality. This island race was among the world's most endangered species. It was down to only ten birds early this century, but captive breeding has placed it in a secure position. However, the problem may recur if not enough people continue to care for this charming little duck.

The species does well on the usual diet of grain and pelleted food, plus greens.

The Laysan Teal can be bred naturally or by artificial incubation, and the ducklings rear easily, becoming remarkably tame. This species is a good mixer and has the added advantage of not requiring vast areas of water.

A male **Lyson Teal**. This charming species is endangered, but recovering.

 Ease of care (scale 1–10) 2

 18 in. (45 cm)

 Heating unnecessary

 Good mixer

 Quiet

 6–10 eggs

 24–26 days incubation

Tufted Duck

(Aythya fuligula)

The Tufted Duck breeds throughout most of Europe and winters in Europe, Asia, and Africa. Slate-blue bill and feet, glossy black plumage with green and purple reflections over all, except for gleaming white flanks, and a long crest extending from the crown make the male an instantly recognizable bird. The female is almost entirely brown and has a shorter crest.

The Tufted Duck is a widespread and popular avicultural species. It is hardy and easy to manage, but as a diving duck, needs a good body of water.

The usual diet of grains and greens needs to be supplemented with some animal matter, such as shrimp and perhaps mealworms. The ducklings feed on live insects, but are easily reared.

A male **Tufted Duck** in full plumage, elegantly gliding through the water.

European Goldeneye

(Bucephala clangula)

Black head, mantle, and back, with glossy green reflections, a white patch in front of the gold eye, and the remainder gleaming white make this a very stylish little diving duck. The female is mainly gray with a white collar.

The Goldeneye is a migratory species, like most ducks, but is not abundant. Changes in breeding or overwintering areas could make a sudden difference to its wild status, which is currently stable, and it is therefore important to conserve captive stocks. Not the easiest of ducks to breed, it needs seclusion. The ducklings are easily stressed and need careful management.

A high-protein diet, including trout pellets and some animal matter, will help bring the bird into breeding condition. It does, however, need good, clean, deep running water.

A **European Goldeneye** displaying his stylish markings as he moves over the water.

Similar species

**Bufflehead
Barrow's Goldeneye**

Ease of care (scale 1–10) 2

18 in. (45 cm)

Heating unnecessary

Good mixer

Quiet

6–10 eggs

30 days incubation

English Call Duck

(Domestic)

The Call Duck is the smallest of the domestic duck breeds, developed in England to decoy their wild brethren into the hunter's trap with their loud and persistent call. Usually white, with bright yellow bills and legs, they are also commonly bred in gray, with a number of other variations becoming popular. They have plump round bodies, short bills, and large round heads.

Call Ducks are hardy and easily cared for, although the ducklings can be quite delicate for the first few days. Finely chopped greens on their water and rolled oats will encourage them, with a gradual change to starter crumbs over a period of two weeks. When grown, they will do well on commercial poultry meal, supplemented with grain and greens.

Green or blue eggs are a feature of the breed, and although they are not prolific layers like the

Small and friendly, the engaging **English Call Duck** has a loud voice.

commercial breeds, Call Ducks will produce a surfeit that may be enjoyed by their keeper. This delightful, friendly bird is deservedly popular.

Ease of care (scale 1–10) 1

18 in. (45 cm)

Heating unnecessary

Good mixer

Very noisy

8–10 eggs

28 days incubation

Ease of care (scale 1–10)

 20 in. (50 cm)

 Heating unnecessary

 Good mixer

 Noisy at times

 8–10 eggs

 28 days incubation

Black East Indie Duck

(Domestic)

The East Indie originated in the United States. It has brilliantly iridescent green-black plumage, viewed at its best in bright sunlight. Slightly larger and slimmer than the English Call Duck, the Indie shows white feathers as it ages. To retain the black plumage, the bird should be carefully mated, using only birds that exhibit no white feathers when young. Breeding birds should be checked carefully, especially under the bill.

The East Indie is very hardy and breeds well, often producing a surprising number of eggs, those at the beginning of the season being black, changing to blue-gray toward the end of the laying period. The ducklings are vigorous and more hardy than those of the Call Duck.

Iridescent plumage is a feature of the domestic **Black East Indie Duck**.

 Ease of care (scale 1–10)

 24–29½ in. (60–75 cm)

 Heating unnecessary

 Good mixer

 Quiet

 10–12 eggs

 28 days incubation

White-Crested Duck

(Domestic)

Initially a white duck of a type similar to the commercial Aylesbury Duck, but with a crest on top of the head like a pompom, the Crested is now available in a number of colors. Improved by selective breeding, the crest varies in size and shape. One third of the ducklings hatched lack the crest. Genetics play a lethal part in the breeding of this duck, for the presence of two crest genes causes the affected embryo to die in the shell. Those that hatch have one gene for a crest or two genes for no crest. One fourth of the embryos carry the two genes, and their premature death reduces hatchability by 25%.

Crested ducks are growing in popularity. Hardy, fast growing, and decorative, laying green, blue, or tinted white eggs, they are a useful variety and can also be used as table birds if you have an excess.

The **White-Crested Duck** has a pompom on its head like a French sailor's cap.

Muscovy Duck
(Cairina moschata)

The Muscovy is the odd one out in the list of domesticated ducks, in that it does not trace its ancestry back to the wild Mallard. Indeed, it is considered by some authorities not to be a duck at all, rather a link between ducks and geese. Muscovies are available in white, black with white forewings, fawn, blue, and pied. Both sexes have an area of rough red skin on their faces, with the much larger drakes also having a fleshy knob at the base of their bill and a small erectile crest. The birds are practically mute, drakes producing little more than a soft hiss.

Unlike other ducks, they are not totally water-proof, and if forced to stay on water for a long time they will drown. Also, unlike other domestic ducks, they can fly, although the drakes often become too heavy to do so. They forage well and are also grazers in the manner of geese. The females are very good mothers and often hide to incubate their large clutch, returning home with a brood of up to 20 ducklings, which they will bravely protect from all predators.

These large ducks need plenty of space, so small yards are not suitable, especially bearing in mind this duck's propensity to fly around its territory. Weighing up to 10 lb. (4.5 kg) at 16 weeks old, Muscovies are highly prized for their lean meat, and the large numbers of young may be reared for the table.

South American in origin, the **Muscovy Duck** is a widespread and popular species.

Ease of care (scale 1–10) 1

22 in. (55 cm)

Heating unnecessary

Good mixer

Quiet

10–20 eggs

33–35 days incubation

Birds of Prey

Until quite recently, it was almost unheard of for hawks, falcons, and buzzards to be even considered as potential breeding birds. Owls had been captive bred for many years, but in relatively low numbers. More recently, captive birds of prey tended to be kept only by falconers who flew them as game hawking birds, the only other keepers generally being zoos and wildlife rescue centers. With the advent of laws forbidding the taking of most birds of prey from the wild almost anywhere in the world, it fell to falconers to try to breed their own if they wished to continue to fly them. Thus hawk breeding took off.

A popular choice for the falconer, the **Harris Hawk** is a sociable and vocal bird.

Now many species are held in good numbers, with some being difficult to find homes for – this applies especially to owls. Breeding hawks, buzzards, and falcons remains a complex affair. In some areas, only registered and licensed keepers are allowed to hold these species as captive birds and must pass strict examinations before doing so. However, as breeding becomes more frequent, and more beginners show real interest, the practice can only expand.

The law regarding the keeping and breeding of birds of prey within the United States is governed by both state and federal laws. Most keepers of birds of prey must be licensed and, as novices, work with a nominated Master Falconer before they can own a bird. Various examinations must then be passed under the guidance of a sponsor or tutor before ownership of birds can be expanded from beginner species. The taking of wild birds is permitted under license in some species, with such birds being used only for falconry purposes. The birds so taken must be immature birds that have left the nest, avoiding imprinting and allowing lost birds to return to the breeding population. To expand into breeding requires a different set of permits. Trading of many species is not allowed, even when captive bred. Because of the system of laws in the United States, it is recommended that the beginner check with the local Fish and Wildlife office before embarking on the keeping and breeding of any species of bird of prey. In Europe, the only native wild birds that may be held in captivity are disabled. However, a license is not required to keep birds of prey, and only a few species have to be registered, although all must be close rung (a closed circular band is put around the bird's ankle when young so that it cannot slip off when the bird grows to adult size).

Where birds of prey differ greatly from other birds is that some are too nervous and intolerant of people to breed unless special conditions are provided. Most falcons and all the accipiters can only be safely kept in aviaries that have no wire

This female **Red-Tailed Hawk** is an impressive sight. Like all birds of prey, it should be handled with respect.

sides. Chambers rather than aviaries, these enclosures are referred to as "skylight/seclusion" aviaries. Constructed with solid sides and a double-wired roof, the chamber cuts out all sight of people and ground level activity that may panic these ultra-sensitive birds. In this way the birds are not on display; the purpose of the chamber is to breed the birds, which generally remain there the whole time. There is, however, an increasing demand for imprinted falcons, and such birds are sufficiently steady to breed. Most buzzards and owls will breed in the more normal type of aviary, although they will do better if they are given some form of seclusion. I have found it best to enclose three sides of the aviary. Because many species are either very nervous or extremely territorial, it is usual not to enter the aviary from the onset of breeding condition until after the breeding cycle has been completed – seven or eight months.

Food for all these birds takes the form of dead animals or birds, and unless some method is established by which leftover items can be removed, conditions soon become smelly and disgusting, and attract flies and other vermin. A regime must be set up to overcome the problem before it arises. Aside from this, birds of prey are remarkably easy to care for in an aviary and, once established, become willing and regular breeders.

Most diurnal birds of prey will nest on a platform. Owls are more variable in their requirements and many need nest boxes, while some nest on the ground. The favored nest site for many breeders is a wooden platform with a large tire forming the outside of a stick nest, the size depending on the species. I prefer a platform made of a strong welded mesh base that sags toward the center, forming a natural cup. A premade nest of sticks – birch, apple, or hazel tree thinnings – made into bundles and wired into a circle will allow the birds to add to the structure. The natural cup is lined with carpet to stop egg damage if the nest bottom becomes thin. The slight spring to the wire platform gives the nest a more natural feeling from the bird's point of view.

7 Ease of care (scale 1–10)

10¼ –14 in. (26–35 cm)

Planted aviary

Heating unnecessary

Keep alone or as pair

Noisy at times

3–6 eggs

35 days incubation

Sparrowhawk

(Accipiter nisus)

This small member of the family of true hawks is typical of all accipiters in that it is excessively nervous and highly strung. None of the accipiters are steady enough ever to be put into open aviaries, and breeding them is fraught with difficulty. Skylight/seclusion aviaries are a must. Any birds produced are generally taken at an early age, imprinted on people, and flown; but they are one of the most demanding birds in falconry. This species is one that will quickly revert to the wild state if left for even a short period. Often better results are obtained by breeding from imprinted birds.

The difference in size between males and females is greater than in any other bird, the females being often more than twice the weight of the males. The usual female weight is around 8 oz. (225 g), but some reach 12 oz. (340 g). Males vary from 4–5½ oz. (115–160 g). This leads to a problem establishing breeding pairs, as an incompatible female will simply eat her potential mate.

There is considerable variation in plumage, depending greatly on age. A mature male is dark slate gray above with a white spot on the nape; flight feathers and tail are dark brown and barred; the underparts are rufous barred; and there are strong reddish tinges to the flanks and sides of the face. The bill is bluish horn, and cere (base of the upper beak) and legs are yellow. As males mature, they tend to become more blue on the back, and the eyes darken from orange to ruby red. Females, while obviously larger, are browner, and the underparts are gray rather than rufous. The eyes are yellow, darkening to pale orange. Young birds tend to be similar to the female, but streaked across the breast rather than barred. Very often the streaks take the form of each breast feather having a tiny "bleeding heart," perhaps as a memorial to all the birds that died to feed it.

I have found the best design for Sparrowhawk aviaries to be an 18 × 12-ft. (5.5 × 3.7-m) L shape with one end heavily planted to give the male the opportunity to hide if the need arises. A nest platform at least 3 ft. (1 m) square with a premade rim of larch twigs is favored.

A sign of breeding condition is the fanning out of the white undertail coverts of the male, loud calling, and also his being the first to feed. All offspring must be close rung at around 12 days.

This species is a specialist bird eater and a diet of day-old chick culls, half-grown quail, or pigeon is preferred. Feeding is carried out through a chute to avoid disturbing the birds.

Similar species

**Goshawk
Cooper's Hawk
Sharp-Shinned Hawk**

A female **Sparrowhawk** in her nest, anxiously guarding her downy chicks.

European Buzzard

(Buteo buteo)

A typical example of a **European Buzzard**, with chocolate brown coloring.

T he buzzard family are often quite difficult to describe with regard to their color, for they range from almost white to almost black. Usually they are dark chocolate brown above, interspersed with black, white, and pale brown. The legs and cere are yellowish, and the eyes are brown, paler when immature. The sexes are alike, the female usually larger, though large males are often bigger than small females. Most hawk keepers tend to weigh their birds as a guide to sex (and also to flying condition) but, behavior apart, the only certain way is to have the birds DNA tested.

Buzzards will breed readily in an open aviary of 12 × 9 ft. (3.7 × 2.7 m), although a larger one is preferred, and once settled will raise a clutch of chicks every year for many years. A larger version of the Sparrowhawk nest platform is used, although I prefer to use a long shelf at the rear of the aviary rather than a square. This gives the chicks room to exercise without falling off the nest. Diet includes day-old chick culls and rats.

Similar species

Swainson's Hawk

Ease of care (scale 1–10) 2

16½ in. (42 cm)

Planted aviary

Heating unnecessary

Keep alone or as pair

Noisy at times

2–4 eggs

35 days incubation

Red-Tailed Hawk

(Buteo jamaicensis)

L ike the European Buzzard, this bird is an extremely variable species, both in size and color. I have had specimens ranging in weight from 1 lb. 12 oz. to 5 lb. 2 oz. (790 g – 2.3 kg). Color is most usually a warm brown above a white breast with a dark belly band and a brick-red tail. Eye color darkens from pale to dark brown with age. Subadults that have achieved their adult red tail often give their junior status away by their eye color. There are several subspecies, with plumage varying from almost black to almost white, with some partial albinism.

In its native North America, this is the most widespread and abundant diurnal bird of prey, a species that may be taken from the wild under license while immature (with a brown barred tail), but only after fledging. Imprinted Red-Tailed Hawks can be quite dangerous to handle.

The Red-Tailed will breed in an open-fronted aviary, or a full wire aviary if given a degree of seclusion. A large, deep nest platform is required, strongly supported and at least 4 ft. (1.2 m) square. It is better, as with the European Buzzard, to give the chicks room to exercise and play. Diet is as for the European Buzzard.

Similar species

Ferruginous Hawk

Ease of care (scale 1–10) 3

18–20 in. (45–50 cm)

Bare aviary

Heating unnecessary

Keep alone or as pair

Noisy at times

2–4 eggs

35 days incubation

A large female **Red-Tailed Hawk**, mistress of all she surveys.

Harris Hawk

(Parabuteo unicinctus)

3 Ease of care (scale 1–10)
16 in. (40 cm)
Bare aviary
Heating unnecessary
Keep alone or as pair
Very noisy
4 eggs
34 days incubation

Generally referred to by ornithologists as the Bay-Winged Hawk, this species is currently far and away the most popular of the birds used for falconry. It is almost naturally tame, appears to actually like people, will fly in company with one or more of its species when hunting, provided it knows them well enough, and is probably the easiest bird of all to fly, making it nearly perfect as a beginner's bird. The only problem for most beginners is the relatively high cost, although that too is falling as more birds are bred.

Color is dark brown above, with chestnut wing linings, shoulder patches, and thighs. The white tail has a very broad black band, making up half the tail. Immatures have a pale streaked breast. Eyes are dark, and there is a patch of bare orange-yellow skin on the face. Cere and legs are yellow.

As with most larger hawks, breeding is not usual until the third or fourth year but, once established, pairs will produce three rounds in one season, especially if manipulated by egg pulling and recycling. The species is very vocal, especially when confronted by dogs, and its harsh call can be quite grating. This is not a bird to keep if you have close and sensitive neighbors.

Diet consists of day-old chicks culls, quail, rats, and pigeons.

Hailing as it does from the southern states and Mexico, this species should be given protection from extremes of cold.

A fine example of the sociable and extremely popular **Harris Hawk**.

American Kestrel

(Falco sparverius)

2 Ease of care (scale 1–10)
8½ in. (22 cm)
Bare aviary
Heating unnecessary
Keep alone or as pair
Noisy at times
3–5 eggs
31–35 days incubation

A typical female **American Kestrel**, with distinctive barred markings.

The American Kestrel is a smaller and more colorful falcon than the European Kestrel. It is also known in the United States as the "Sparrowhawk," but confusingly bears no relation to the rather lunatic accipiter that bears this name in Britain. The male has blue-gray wings; rusty red tail and back; pale spotted breast; blue, gray, and black barred head; and dark eyes. The female lacks the blue-gray areas and is more heavily barred.

This little falcon is free-breeding, and has been used frequently in a variety of research into falcon reproduction. It will breed in an open aviary if given height, preferring to look down at you rather than be at the same level. An open-fronted nest box is preferred, although a simple platform with a sand base may be used. In common with other falcons, no nest material is used.

A diet of day-old chick culls may be supplemented with small quail, mealworms, or beetles.

Similar species

European Kestrel

Peregrine Falcon

(Falco peregrinus)

A formidable **Peregrine Falcon** resting on a ledge. This is the world's fastest living bird.

The Peregrine is one of the great falcons. When trained as a falconry bird, its placid and beguiling behavior, coupled with its grace and speed, encourage all who handle it to revere it above all things. As a wild bird it seeks to avoid humans, so when it is kept as a breeding bird there is normally little or no hope of producing chicks other than in seclusion breeding chambers (but see below). The bird was first bred at Cornell University by Tom Cade, who hit upon this system and saved the bird from certain extinction in the United States with his breeding and release scheme.

The male has slate-gray upper parts with dark bars. The crown and cheeks are very dark, black in some individuals, with a prominent mustachial streak giving the bird an "executioner's hood." Eyes are dark; the cere and feet yellow. The female is one-third larger in overall body size, though not in length, and is darker and with heavier bars. In immature plumage the birds are brown, and the underparts are streaked rather than barred as in the adults.

If the female is imprinted upon its keeper, by deliberate hand rearing and encouragement of sexual behavior as the bird matures, breeding is much easier to achieve and an aviary may not even be required. Such birds have been artificially inseminated, laid eggs, and hatched and reared chicks even while leashed to a falconry block perch. I once saw a female Peregrine rearing three young of her own, together with five young Merlins who had been orphaned.

Similar species

Gyr Falcon
Saker Falcon
Lanner Falcon
Prairie Falcon
Luggar Falcon

Ease of care (scale 1–10) 5

12½–16 in. (32–40 cm)

Bare aviary

Heating unnecessary

Keep alone or as pair

Noisy at times

3–4 eggs

35 days incubation

Ease of care
(scale 1–10)
1

18–26 in.
(45–65 cm)

Planted
aviary

Heating
unnecessary

Keep alone
or as pair

Noisy
at times

2–3 eggs

35 days
incubation

European Eagle Owl

(Bubo bubo)

This huge owl is quite variable in size, depending on its origins. It is found in Scandinavia, most of Europe except Britain, and Asia and North Africa in a number of variable subspecies. Generally, the farther south they are, the smaller and paler they become. The Finnish and Siberian birds are undoubtedly the world's largest owl, and individuals may weigh in excess of 9 lb. (4 kg). One look at the massive feet and claws will leave you with no doubt that it is also an extremely powerful bird. To enter an aviary where this species is in breeding condition without protective clothing would be most unwise.

Color is a mix of black and brown stripes and bars on a pale brown ground. The round face with large orange eyes is topped by two mobile ear tufts, which are used to indicate mood. The legs and huge feet are feathered right to the base of the long black talons. The sexes are identical in color, but the female is usually slightly larger. The female has a deeper call, but you need to have a comparison to be certain. Careful observation or surgical sexing may be the only way to determine the sex of some individuals.

Breeding may be carried out in a large open aviary with some seclusion close to the preferred nest site. I like my birds to have an aviary large enough for the birds to at least fly in a circle. With such a large owl the turning circle is around 18 ft. (5.5 m). A few small conifers and ground cover plants may be planted, especially if the aviary is a good size; but not near the perches, because the droppings will quickly kill any living plant. As a general rule, this owl will nest on the ground with the male making the nest scrape, for no nest material is used. It will, however, use a nest box or high platform. Breeding begins early, often in January. Incubation is around 35 days from the date of the first egg, hatching being staggered in typical owl fashion. Established pairs can be embarrassingly free-breeding.

Once mature the bird can be quite vocal and, since it calls most at night, you should give thought to your neighbors. Happily, the call of the European, while it does carry a long way, is not particularly loud. It utters its scientific name, *Bubo* (or *Uhu*, which is its German name) – the only bird I know that does. I think the call is wonderful – but I am just a little biased.

The diet may include chick culls, but the birds do best on rats and rabbits. In the wild, this owl is said to kill and eat all creatures, avian and mammalian, up to the size of small roe deer.

Similar species

Turkmenian Eagle Owl

The **European Eagle Owl** has distinctive orange eyes and is the largest of all owls.

Great Horned Owl

(Bubo virginianus)

A **Great Horned Owl** displaying its beautiful mottled plumage as it rests.

The Great Horned Owl, the largest American owl by weight rather than by overall length, is also the most widespread, found from northern Canada down to Tierra del Fuego at the extreme tip of South America. There are 17 subspecies. The plumage is a mix of richly mottled brown, white, buff, and black on the upper parts, and a buff underside with darker barring. A reddish facial disk is bordered by a dark line, and there are large, expressive ear tufts. This is the familiar "hoot owl" of American childhood, and the owl of cartoons. In reality it is an extremely powerful predator, and in breeding condition it needs to be treated with considerable respect.

Breeding starts early, with courtship beginning in January. A shelf or nest platform is preferred, with a readymade stick nest. The six or seven-note hoot, with pairs calling antiphonally for hours, can be a problem during the breeding season. The young are slow to develop, but often leave the nest and clamber about before they can fly.

Diet is as for the European Eagle Owl.

Ease of care (scale 1–10) 2

18 in. (45 cm)

Planted aviary

Heating unnecessary

Keep alone or as pair

Noisy at times

2–3 eggs

30–35 days incubation

Bengal Eagle Owl

(Bubo bengalensis)

The Bengal Eagle Owl is a single species found in northern and central India. It is smaller and paler than the European Eagle Owl, but otherwise similar.

One of the most popular owls in captivity, it is intelligent (most owls are not), attractive, and entertaining, being relatively active and inquisitive. The bird likes to sunbathe as well as bathe, and is rather less wooden during the day than most. Early evening is the time to watch the large owls; the Bengal likes the stimulus afforded by anything it can pick up and throw around, practicing killing techniques on sticks, stones, and feathers.

Breeding often begins in November, and eggs are laid in a ground scrape. Once established, pairs will breed regularly for many years.

Similar species

African Spotted Eagle Owl

The **Bengal Eagle Owl** is a very popular owl, despite its fierce orange eyes.

Ease of care (scale 1–10) 2

14–16 in. (35–40 cm)

Planted aviary

Heating unnecessary

Keep alone or as pair

Noisy at times

2–3 eggs

32 days incubation

1
Ease of care
(scale 1–10)

11 in.
(28 cm)

Bare
aviary

Heating
unnecessary

Keep alone
or as pair

Noisy
at times

5–10 eggs

29 days
incubation

Barn Owl

(Tyto alba)

The Barn Owl, also known as the White or Screech Owl, is the most widespread of all land birds, found on every continent in around 35 subspecies. It has a buff and ash-gray back of intricate markings, and a white front and under-wing area. The legs and feet are sparsely feathered. A heart-shaped facial disk and very dark button eyes make this bird a stunningly beautiful creature.

Although the bird is seriously endangered as a wild species in Britain, it is embarrassingly fecund as a breeding bird in captivity, and it is now considered irresponsible to allow Barn Owls to breed unrestricted. Pairs can produce up to 20 offspring in a single year, which themselves are mature at nine months. Most breeders now only allow a part clutch to be produced, pricking eggs or replacing them with dummies.

The **Barn Owl** is a bird of great beauty with an elegant white face.

Breeding will take place in any month. Chicks hatch every other day to produce a range of ages from almost fully grown down to tiny babies, all of which normally survive if the food supply is constant. Diet is day-old chick culls and mice.

4
Ease of care
(scale 1–10)

6¼ in.
(16 cm)

Planted
aviary

Heating
unnecessary

Keep alone
or as pair

Noisy
at times

4–5 eggs

29 days
incubation

Little Owl

(Athene noctua)

There are 14 subspecies of this small, yellow-eyed, and delightfully grumpy-looking owl. Widespread throughout southern Europe, Asia, and Africa, it was not found in Britain until introduced in the late 19th century, since which time it has expanded to become that country's second most numerous owl species. Hunting both by night and day, it lives largely on beetles, worms, and some small birds. It is more often heard than seen.

Upper parts are grayish-brown, spotted, mottled, and barred with white. The spots form streaks on the head and a distinctive eyebrow. Whitish underparts are streaked with brown. The sexes are identical, with a predominance of males.

Breeding begins in April. The bird prefers a nest box. Pairs are often difficult to establish and many never lay. I had one bird for seven years before she laid an egg. The chicks are a delight; gray tennis balls on pipecleaner legs.

A charming example of a mottled **Little Owl**, perching on a wooden post.

Tawny Owl

(Strix aluco)

Found throughout Europe and Asia as far as Japan, this bird is a typical Strix species. Quite variable in its coloration, it has two distinct phases, a gray and a rufous. The latter is the more common, being a warm reddish buff mottled with dark brown. Pale tips to the secondaries form white bars on the wings. A gray facial disk is bordered with brown, and the eyes are very dark. The feet and legs are densely feathered.

Very much nocturnal, the Tawny Owl is the most numerous British species, familiar as the owl with the long, quivering call, often written as "To-wit, to-woo." In fact the female calls "Kee-vik" and the male responds with the hooting "To-woo."

Breeding, which is often spasmodic, begins in April. The bird likes a deep box, although a platform nest will be used if it is secluded.

The timid **Tawny Owl** is very definitely a nocturnal creature. It is often difficult to breed.

Similar species

Barred Owl

 Ease of care (scale 1–10) 3

 8½ in. (22 cm)

 Bare aviary

 Heating unnecessary

 Keep alone or as pair

 Noisy at times

 3–4 eggs

 30 days incubation

Scops Owl

(Otus scops)

This quite small owl, found from Russia to Taiwan, is one of several subspecies and a vast array of other related species. Similar in color to the Little Owl, it is distinguished immediately by its hornlike ear tufts. Very nocturnal, it is difficult to spot by day, and draws itself up straight and erects its ear tufts if disturbed.

Bred in low numbers at present, it is relatively expensive, but may soon become more readily available. The bird is highly insectivorous and besides mice and day-old chick culls it will take crickets and other insects.

It is highly vocal with a monotonous call, well known to anyone who visits southern Europe during the summer. The bird will nest in a box or on a well-hidden sand-covered platform.

Similar species

White-Faced Scops Owl
Collared Scops Owl

 Ease of care (scale 1–10) 5

 6 in. (15 cm)

 Planted aviary

 Heating unnecessary

 Keep alone or as pair

 Noisy at times

 3–4 eggs

 38 days incubation

Another very nocturnal owl, the **Scops** is gaining in popularity.

Burrowing Owl

(Athene cunicular)

- 4 Ease of care (scale 1–10)
- 8¾ in. (22 cm)
- Bare aviary
- Heating unnecessary
- Keep alone or as pair
- Noisy at times
- 2–6 eggs
- 29 days incubation

This small owl of the open prairie is very similar to the European Little Owl, except for the length of its legs. Taking refuge from the vicious heat of the summer in its native North America, this bird spends much of its time underground. Most of its time on the surface is spent on the ground, where it uses its long legs to extend its field of view rather than perch.

Endangered in many parts of its range, it has been bred in considerable numbers in captivity, and is fast approaching the stage in some countries where its numbers will become an embarrassment. It can be quite expensive to buy, despite the large numbers being bred.

Generally, Burrowing Owls do not do much burrowing themselves if they can help it, and a system of pipes laid under a mound will suit them well. In the wild they inhabit the tunnels of the Prairie Dog, a burrowing rodent.

A single **Burrowing Owl**, seen typically on the ground where it spends most of its time.

Great Gray Owl

(Strix nebulosa)

- 4 Ease of care (scale 1–10)
- 18 in. (45 cm)
- Planted aviary
- Heating unnecessary
- Keep alone or as pair
- Quiet
- 2–6 eggs
- 35 days incubation

The look of this beautiful large North American owl is spoiled for me by the feeling that its eyes are too small and too close together. That aside, the bird is a wonderful soft mix of mottled gray, brown, and white, with a large facial disk of concentric dark rings surrounding bright yellow eyes. Two thin white marks under the bill give the impression of a white mustache or collar. Very lightly built with a large amount of feathers, it looks much larger than it really is. Mostly feeding on small rodents, it has remarkable hearing, often locating prey at considerable distances in deep snow.

It has now become established as a breeding species, although it is still in low numbers so that it remains expensive. It likes a stick nest platform or an open-fronted nest box.

This bird has little fear of humans, but is still quite secretive and needs some seclusion. A diet of rats, mice, and chick culls is required.

The rare **Great Gray Owl** is actually quite small but is covered with large feathers.

Long-Eared Owl

(Asio otis)

Found in Europe, Canada, and Africa, this is a very secretive owl, relatively sparsely distributed, and generally confined to fir woodland. The adult bird is a dark marbled gray and brown over

A **Long-Eared Owl** at rest, with its ear tufts standing erect. This owl is rare in captivity.

buff with black streaks. The facial disk is buff, darker close to the yellow eyes. The underparts are streaked buff and brown with dusky bars forming crosses or arrows. At rest the long ear tufts from which the bird gains its name are held erect, almost touching at the points. It is quite vocal, with a long drawn-out hoot, totally unlike that of the Tawny Owl. A series of barks and wing claps in flight are also recorded.

Not an easy species to breed, it usually takes to a preformed stick nest on a wire platform, but in spite of being offered a number of alternative sites, it may just nest on the ground.

Although usually fed day-old chick culls, it prefers a diet of small rats and mice.

Similar species

Short-Eared Owl

 Ease of care (scale 1–10) 7

 9½ in. (24 cm)

 Planted aviary

 Heating unnecessary

 Keep alone or as pair

 Noisy at times

 3–5 eggs

 32 days incubation

Snowy Owl

(Nyctea scandiaca)

Two charming female **Snowy Owls**, displaying their distinctive gray markings.

As the name indicates, this is a bird of Arctic and circumpolar range. The males are white with a few gray-brown marks, while the larger females are more heavily marked, as are the immatures once fully feathered. The chicks may be sexed once they are feathered up, for the males have three bars on the tail, while the females have five. The feet are heavily feathered right down to the talons, and only the soles are bare. The eyes are bright yellow. Initially grayish white, the chicks soon develop a dark gray down with white feet, giving the appearance of wearing socks.

This species nests on the ground, often right in the open, scorning any form of protection or seclusion. They are quick to mature and can produce embarrassingly large numbers of offspring.

Care must be exercised with the covering of the aviary floor, which should be of soft sand or a sand and peat mixture. Snowy Owls suffer badly from bumble foot (a disease of the sole of the foot caused by infection) if kept on a hard surface, but the chicks quickly succumb to aspergillosis if hay and straw are used to soften the floor.

 Ease of care (scale 1–10) 1

 16–18 in. (40–45 cm)

 Bare aviary

 Heating unnecessary

 Keep alone or as pair

 Quiet

 12 eggs

 35 days incubation

Pigeons and Doves

The two names mean the same, and many pigeons and doves have alternative names; for example, the Wood Pigeon is often called the Ring Dove. There are close to 400 species of pigeons. The domestic pigeon in most of its forms, be it a racer or a show variety, is descended from the Rock Dove (*Columba livia*), as are the millions of feral pigeons that inhabit our towns and cities.

Most species are grain feeders, simple to cater for and peaceful with other species, although a significant number are fruit eaters — usually these are larger and more troublesome breeds. Pigeons are less peaceful toward their own species and often need to be housed in single pairs only, with offspring removed as soon as they are independent, lest they should be killed by their parents. The line between love and hate is a fine one.

A **Crested Pigeon**, with its unmistakable pointed crest and bright orange eyes.

Diamond Dove

(Geopelia cuneata)

In the normal color variety, the Diamond Dove is a pale blue gray on head, breast, and neck, with the back and wings gray brown. The underside is white, and the wings are spotted with white. The sexes are similar but a red patch around the eye is larger and more obvious in the male, which also has a greater amount of spotting on the wings. There is a growing number of attractive color mutations, including fawn, silver, and blue.

Found in northern and some parts of central Australasia, this species is the most widely kept and popular of all the exotic pigeons and doves. It can lay claim to being domesticated, and is so free-breeding that I have seen pairs attempting to rear chicks in the feed dishes of pet-store cages.

These doves are peaceful toward every species except their own, and chicks need to be removed when independent. A diet of small canary seeds, millet, and a little hemp, plus green food, will keep Diamonds in good order. They will build a flimsy stick nest in any shallow receptacle.

The **Diamond Dove** typically has gray markings, but other colors are also available.

Ease of care (scale 1–10) 1

7 in. (18 cm)

Bare aviary

Heating unnecessary

Good mixer

Quiet

2 eggs

13–14 days incubation

Zebra Dove

(Geopelia striata)

This dove is rather more widespread in its distribution than the Diamond, covering Borneo, New Guinea, Burma, Thailand, and western Australia. Reasonably common in most of its natural range, it has been introduced into Hawaii. It is similarly colored to the Diamond, except that the wings are barred black, while the sides of the neck, breast, and flanks have black and white barring. The sexes are similar, but the female is smaller and paler.

This bird can be very free-breeding and hardy, and is a charming alternative to the more widely known Diamond Dove.

A **Zebra Dove** fluffed up against the cold. It is a popular species, and easy to care for.

Ease of care (scale 1–10) 1

7¾ in. (20 cm)

Bare aviary

Heating unnecessary

Good mixer

Quiet

2 eggs

14 days incubation

Ease of care (scale 1–10)

11 in. (28 cm)

Planted aviary

Heating unnecessary

Good mixer

Quiet

2 eggs

14 days incubation

Senegal Dove

(Streptopelia sengalensis)

This attractive **Senegal Dove** is displaying its soft brownish-red breast.

Found in many areas of North Africa, and from the southern edge of the Sahara down to Cape Province, this dove is also known as the Laughing Dove, from its soft, attractive coo. The upper surface is a soft brown, with the back, wings, and rump gray. The sides of the neck are a deep reddish brown with black spots. The undersurface is pale vinous red fading to white.

The species can be very free-breeding if you have a true pair. Behavior is no indicator of sex, other than the production of eggs. They are laid in a flimsy nest, and the adults will often start a second brood before the first is independent. The first chicks must be removed as soon as they can feed; otherwise, their father may kill them.

They are easily managed and hardy, and require a simple diet of canary seeds and millet with buckwheat, hemp, split maize, plus green food and gravel.

Similar species

Chinese Necklace Dove

Ease of care (scale 1–10)

7 ¾ in. (20 cm)

Planted aviary

Some heat required

Good mixer

Quiet

2 eggs

14 days incubation

Tambourine Dove

(Turtur tympanistria)

This pair of **Tambourine Doves** show the subtle differences in the two sexes' coloration.

This striking small dove from southern Africa is dark brown above with dark blue spots on the wings, and white forehead and underparts. The female has gray in place of white, and less obvious wing spots.

While the species is common in its range, it is not often imported. It is worthwhile, for it is easy to sex and will often breed quite freely. Almost as often, however, it will not, which makes each pair something of a gamble. Although they are usually quiet and confident aviary birds, they do require seclusion if they are to succeed in breeding. They are not entirely hardy and are best kept indoors in frost-free accommodations in winter.

A diet of canary seeds and millet with green food and gravel is required. Birds will also take some live food, such as mealworms.

Similar species

Black-Billed Wood Dove
Blue-Spotted Wood Dove

Namaqua Dove

(Oena capensis)

Ease of care
(scale 1–10)

9 in.
(23 cm)

Planted
aviary

Some heat
required

Good
mixer

Quiet

2 eggs

14 days
incubation

A pair of **Namaqua Doves**. The female, without the black mask, is often hard to find.

Also known as the Masked or Cape Dove, this small bird is found over a considerable area of central and eastern Africa, together with Madagascar and Cape Province, where it prefers hot and dry areas. The upper surfaces are gray brown, with a black mask covering the face and throat. There are blue wing spots, dark bands on the rump, and a long graduated tail. The female lacks the black mask.

This is quite a delicate species and, although frequently available, needs careful handling at first. A sheltered aviary is best, with a number of nest baskets from which to choose a site, tucked into cover. They do not like dampness and do better in a dry summer. They take time to settle when imported, often several years. I had one pair for four years before they suddenly decided to breed, following which they were difficult to stop.

Although most doves produce a "pigeon pair" – one chick of each sex – this species seems to have set out to break the mold and males predominate.

Ease of care (scale 1–10) — 2

 10 in. (25 cm)

 Planted aviary

 Heating unnecessary

 Good mixer

 Quiet

 2 eggs

 14 days incubation

Emerald Dove

(Chalcophaps indica)

This male **Emerald Dove** is distinguishable by his white eyebrow.

Found in much of southeastern Asia, India, and through the islands to northern Australia, this pigeon is a colorful bird with a metallic green mantle and wings, a blue-gray nape and crown, a black back, and a vinaceous red underside. The male has a white eyebrow, which is lacking in the female of the species.

Becoming rarer in some parts of its range, it is still fairly abundant in most areas and frequently available. It is completely hardy once established and can be free-breeding. A platform or shelf will be used as the base of the nest, but I have had them nest on top of other species' nests, which can be a nuisance. To overcome this, I have allowed plenty of alternative sites. The higher the better seems to be the rule, although this bird spends a great deal of time on the ground.

The bird likes a diet of canary seeds and millet, together with buckwheat, hemp, and cracked corn, together with some live food and berries.

 Ease of care (scale 1–10) — 4

 10 in. (25 cm)

 Planted aviary

 Some heat required

 Good mixer

 Quiet

2 eggs

16 days incubation

Luzon Bleeding-Heart Pigeon

(Gallicolumba luzonica)

A highly prized and relatively rare species in aviculture, this bird now has an international stud book listing. It is gray-brown above with a suffusion of metallic green and purple, the cheeks, throat, and breast white with a patch of bright red in the center of the breast. The belly and abdomen are yellow. The female is similar, but the red "bleeding heart" from which the species derives its name is smaller.

This species does best in a planted aviary with ground cover. The males are often very pugnacious, and the hens need cover to hide. Even established pairs can be difficult, and care is needed.

A diet of canary and millet seeds, buckwheat, hemp, and cracked corn needs to be supplemented with a commercial insectivorous food, live food, such as mealworm, ant eggs, and some berries. The birds can become very tame. Mixing well with other small birds, they can breed freely.

The tell-tale "bleeding heart" can easily be seen on this rare **Luzon Pigeon**.

Garden Fantail

(Domestic)

This pigeon is derived from the Rock Dove, *Columba livia*, and like its wild progenitor is a flock bird. It is usually white but, frequently mismated with feral pigeons, it also comes in the blues and grays of the familiar city pigeon. Where it varies is in the tail which, instead of the normal 12 feathers, often has as many as 24, forming an inverted V rather than the full spread fan of the true exhibition fantail pigeon.

Garden Fantails are usually established in a pigeon coop, either mounted on a pole or set under the gable of a house as a decorative feature. When setting up Fantails, it is best to keep them enclosed with a temporary aviary of light netting around their coop until they begin to breed, which is usually within a few weeks of arrival. Depending on the size of the coop and the ultimate size of the flock you wish to maintain, two or three pairs make a good basis. It is useful to set up the coop in such a way as to be able to reach the nest holes. The birds will breed continuously if they are unchecked and your four birds can very quickly become 44.

They are an attractive addition to any garden if controlled, and, although I do not advocate this, I have seen flocks dyed various colors with food dye, which makes an amazing sight when they are flying free together.

An attractive free-flying **Garden Fantail**, often seen on rooftops.

Ease of care (scale 1–10) 1

18 in. (45 cm)

Cage

Heating unnecessary

Good mixer

Noisy at times

2 eggs

18 days incubation

Pheasants and Quail

The large family Phasianidae ranges in size from the tiny Chinese Painted Quail to the giant Argus Pheasant and the Indian Peafowl. It includes some 180 species, mainly from temperate and tropical regions. They are not easy to divide into natural groups, but quail are found in both the Old World and the New, while the true pheasants are absent from the New World, except where they have been introduced. A less glamorous member of the pheasant clan is the domestic chicken, bred from Southeast Asian jungle fowl.

Some species are well established outside their native range. The Common Pheasant is reared in its millions as a game bird, and the Japanese Quail is domesticated for its eggs and meat. Bobwhites have moved into inner cities in the United States where, freed from the pressure of hunting, they are a familiar sight. The California Quail was introduced into New Zealand, where it is now common in parks and open sheep country. In Britain, such releases have often taken place in the past with species such as the Golden Pheasant, but are now prohibited by the Wildlife and Countryside Act.

The smaller species are often quite peaceable and will live happily and unobtrusively in a mixed collection, but some of the larger ones can definitely be kept only as a single species. Many pheasants have well-developed spurs on their legs and are not averse to using them. Male Silver Pheasants, for example, are notorious for attacking anything that moves when they are in breeding condition. Most pheasants will do well on a diet consisting largely of grain and pellet foods, but they do need space. Quail often do well in small units, although they show off better in planted aviaries. Gravel is generally essential, and if they are eating unhusked grain, they will certainly require sharp sand to aid digestion.

A beautiful example of a **Reeves Pheasant**, now an endangered species. These birds need plenty of space.

Chinese Painted Quail

(Excalfactoria chinensis)

The smallest of the quail, this species is found in Southeast Asia and Australia. There are now many color mutations, but the normal form is still the most colorful – brown above with darker streaks, blue-gray on the cheeks and back, and deep chestnut on the lower breast and abdomen. There is a black line bordered with white on the throat and under the eye. Females are uniform brown with streaking, and lack the male's chestnut belly and blue flanks.

The most widely kept of all the avicultural species of quail, these are very hardy and do well in a garden aviary, provided they have shelter from rain and frost. They are particularly prone to night fright and will explode from the aviary floor if disturbed, damaging themselves in the process and seriously disturbing other sleeping birds.

They have an infuriating habit of laying eggs just where they happen to be standing at the time, so the species has mostly been spread by artificial incubation. This has exacerbated the problem, and it is now difficult to find a strain that will incubate its own eggs. Sometimes it helps to gather up the eggs and place them and the mother in a corner under a wire netting cone. When the eggs hatch, at first the father will feed and guard the whole family, but as soon as the sex of the chicks is evident, he becomes aggressive toward the young males.

Most keepers put the birds on the floor to clear up waste seeds, which they will do, but they do better if provided with their own mixture of small canary seeds and millets, together with green foods and gravel. They will mix with any species that does not molest them, living on the ground and troubling no one.

A male **Chinese Painted Quail** sheltering in grass. This is a deservedly popular species.

Ease of care (scale 1–10) — 1

5 in. (13 cm)

Planted aviary

Heating unnecessary

Good mixer

Quiet

6–12 eggs

16–17 days incubation

Ease of care
(scale 1–10)

6 in.
(15 cm)

Planted
aviary

Heating
unnecessary

Good
mixer

Quiet

8–12 eggs

17–18 days
incubation

Japanese Quail

(Coturnix japonica)

Although scarcely larger in overall length than the Chinese Quail, the Japanese is perhaps three times the weight. This is the species that is bred for culinary purposes and egg production. Given a minimum day length of 14 hours, the Japanese Quail will lay an egg every day. Japan is only part of its natural range, which extends through Thailand, Laos, and Burma.

A mainly brown bird with dark and light streaks, it has a chin and throat of a dull red. The hens are heavily streaked on the breast, where the males are plain with a reddish-buff tinge. As with the Chinese Quail, it is very difficult to find birds that will incubate their own eggs. If producing by artificial incubation and rearing – which is quite a simple technique – beware of overcrowding, or feather plucking will take place with a vengeance.

Japanese Quail can be kept in flocks, but for avicultural purposes it is best to restrict the group to one cock and five hens. If there is only one hen

An adult male **Japanese Quail**, strutting through foliage.

the cock will tread her incessantly, stripping the feathers from neck and back in the process. Diet is mixed canary seeds and millet, or turkey starter crumbs. Any chicks produced need a very high-protein diet, and enjoy live food. The modern intensively bred birds are mature in 7 weeks.

Ease of care
(scale 1–10)

9½–11 in.
(24–28 cm)

Bare
aviary

Heating
unnecessary

Good
mixer

Noisy
at times

8–12 eggs

17–20 days
incubation

Bobwhite

(Colinus virginianus)

Mainly rufous brown with darker brown spots and streaks, it has a breast and underparts of buffish brown and a distinctive white eye stripe and throat, under which there is a black border-line. Generally abundant throughout its range of the central and eastern United States through to Mexico, this species is also commercially bred, either as a game bird or for culinary purposes.

Breeding is usually by artificial incubation and rearing, as with the Japanese Quail, is quite simple once mastered. The males have an onomatopoeic call "Bob White!" which carries, and can be annoying.

Management is similar to that of the Japanese Quail, but this species is less hardy and should be wintered inside. Like all species of quail, it is unhappy in damp conditions.

This charming **Bobwhite** is well camouflaged against the dry brown grass.

California Quail

(Lophortyx californica)

Mainly gray, with a black and white throat, a chestnut abdomen, and scale-like markings over much of the lower body, this quail has a distinctive black crest. Found in western areas of the United States and Mexico, it is reasonably common and currently increasing.

This bird is hardy and prolific, and will spend more time perching than many of its relatives, which increases its interest. Egg scattering is quite usual, but artificial incubation can quickly increase numbers. Although they are generally safe in mixed company, the males can make life difficult for smaller companions.

Diet should consist of canary seed and chicken or turkey starter crumbs, together with green food. It also enjoys live food.

This **California Quail** is seen here on the ground, but it is equally happy on a perch.

Ease of care (scale 1–10)

10 in. (25 cm)

Bare aviary

Heating unnecessary

May attack smaller birds

Quiet

10–15 eggs

23 days incubation

Scaled Quail

(Callipepla squamata)

This species is also called the Blue Quail, for its plumage is mainly blue gray in color. It has a short crest. The flanks are streaked gray-brown, and the lower breast and abdomen are buff. Females lack the dark streaks on the face and throat. Found in Mexico and the southwestern United States, it is fairly common. As an avicultural species, it is not as widely kept as other quail, but is on the increase.

As the hens do not usually sit on their own eggs, artificial incubation is generally advisable.

Like the California Quail, the Scaled Quail will spend some time perching, roosting as high as possible rather than resting on the ground.

The blue scale-like feathers of the **Scaled Quail** give the bird a metallic look.

Ease of care (scale 1–10)

9½ in. (24 cm)

Planted aviary

Some heat required

Good mixer

Quiet

10–12 eggs

23 days incubation

Ease of care
(scale 1–10)
1

6 in.
(15 cm)

Planted
aviary

Some heat
required

Good
mixer

Quiet

6–8 eggs

16–18 days
incubation

Rain Quail

(Coturnix coromandelica)

A small quail from India, Burma, and Sri Lanka, this warm brown bird has streaks of yellow on upper wing surfaces and back. The breast is buff with a black center and black spots on the flanks. The cheeks and throat are white, and there is a white eye stripe bordered with black.

At one time this quail was very common in aviculture, but is less so now, although interest in quail generally is expanding. It is a nervous species, and care must be taken at night not to disturb roosting birds, which will explode upward. Such actions can be devastating in a mixed aviary. Like the previously described quail species, the Rain Quail is not given to sitting on a clutch.

A typical example of the unusual and now rare **Rain Quail**.

Similar species

Harlequin Quail

Ease of care
(scale 1–10)
4

11 in.
(28 cm)

Planted
aviary

Heating
essential

Good
mixer

Quiet

2–4 eggs

18 days
incubation

Roulroul Partridge

(Rollulus roulroul)

Mostly dark green with metallic blue and purple refractions, a black head with a white patch on the crown, chestnut wings and crest, and an area of naked red skin around the eye, this difficult and delicate partridge is an exceptionally striking bird.

It has never been abundant, but a fair number of captive-bred birds has been offered for sale in recent years. Propagation is generally by artificial means, although pairs will sometimes sit on eggs and rear their chicks. To do so they need cover and tropical warmth. A heated greenhouse used for tropical houseplants is suitable. The birds enjoy dust bathing and will appreciate a sandbox.

Diet should be based on mixed canary seeds and millet, together with a commercial insectivorous mixture, green food, and some live food.

A male **Roulroul Partridge** caring for its chicks. This is a sight to encourage breeders.

Himalayan Monal Pheasant

(Lophophorus impeyanus)

This striking bird has a metallic green head and throat, a green and gold mantle, and dark blue wings with purple refractions. The neck is a copper green, the body and underparts are black, and the tail is bright chestnut.

The bird inhabits the lower slopes of the Himalayas only, where hunting has seriously reduced its numbers. At one time it was considered impossible for small aviculturalists to obtain many of the rarer pheasants, but captive breeding has now made this and other rare species more widely available.

Like most pheasants, the Monal needs space and a degree of privacy. It is best kept in pairs with a dry roosting area and dry sand for dust bathing and digging. The floor, or at least the parts close to the aviary sides, need to be underwired, for the birds will dig their way out in no time.

Breeding is possible with natural incubation if a pair are given the right conditions, and where possible at least one clutch should be reared by the parent birds. Consistently producing birds by artificial means simply expands the problems.

A diet of grains and pheasant pellets, green food, and some live food is required.

The **Himalayan Monal's** plumage is all the more vibrant when seen in sunlight.

Ease of care (scale 1–10) 3

28 in. (70 cm)

Planted aviary

Heating unnecessary

Keep alone or as pair

Quiet

4–6 eggs

28 days incubation

Ease of care
(scale 1–10)
3

33 in.
(85 cm)

Planted
aviary

Heating
unnecessary

Keep alone
or as pair

Quiet

6–8 eggs

25 days
incubation

Siamese Fireback Pheasant

(Lophura diardi)

This female **Siamese Fireback** is well camouflaged against the brown earth.

This species is decreasing in most of its range, which includes Burma, Thailand, and Indochina, but is increasing in aviculture. The head, upper back, and breast are gray with fine black vermiculations. The tail is black with a green sheen, the lower belly breast shines with purple refractions, and the back shines orange and red with the lower portion edged with metallic blue and purple. The face is almost completely covered by a red wattle, and topped with a black crest sweeping from the black head. The female is mainly mottled brown and chestnut, and has no crest.

Relatively hardy, it dislikes damp conditions, and needs frost-free night quarters. The Fireback should be kept in pairs, and is not good with other birds, let alone other pheasants. Plenty of ground cover is required. Most propagation is by artificial incubation. Diet is as for the Monal.

Ease of care
(scale 1–10)
3

35 in.
(90 cm)

Planted
aviary

Heating
unnecessary

Keep alone
or as pair

Quiet

6–10 eggs

25 days
incubation

White Eared Pheasant

(Crossoptilon crossoptilon)

The White Eared Pheasant is just that, almost entirely white. There is a silvery sheen to the wings, and the head and tail are black, while the face is covered with dull red, naked skin. The female is similar but smaller.

Ranging from Tibet to Sichuan, this bird is endangered in the wild, but has been saved by captive breeding programs. It is still quite rare, but stocks are increasing. Breeding is mostly by artificial incubation and rearing. The chicks are relatively simple to rear, but are great peckers of each other, as are the adults. In other ways, the White Eared Pheasant is a quiet and accommodating species and can be allowed to fly free, provided that it is kept safe from predators.

Diet should consist of grains and pheasant pellets with green food, and birds should be given plenty of opportunity to dig for roots and small insects. A good system is to fence in areas of old grass in rotation, which the birds quickly peck rather than dig out.

The **White Eared Pheasant** has a striking red face, black head, and white body.

Reeves Pheasant

(Syrmaticus reevesii)

O ne of the long-tailed pheasants, this attractive bird from China is notably belligerent and needs to be kept as a single species. Most of the upper and lower surfaces are edged with black, the back being copper buff while the underside is a more reddish buff. The crown of the head, throat, and nape are black with varying amounts of white markings. The long tail is banded black, white, and copper brown. The female is paler and has a shorter tail.

A long-established avicultural favorite, the Reeves Pheasant needs a great deal of space to maintain its tail, which in mature birds may be up to 24 in. (60 cm) long. It breeds well, with the females often hatching and rearing their own chicks, though they need to be watched as they grow. The males are extremely aggressive and need more than one female to keep them happy.

Diet is as for the White Eared Pheasant.

Ease of care (scale 1–10)

33 in. (85 cm)

Planted aviary

Heating unnecessary

Keep alone or as pair

Quiet

8–12 eggs

25 days incubation

Reeves Pheasants drink water but bathe in dry sand.

Golden Pheasant

(Chrysolophus pictus)

A fine example of the male **Golden Pheasant's** spectacular plumage.

T his bird's spectacular plumage makes it the best known and most widely kept of all the pheasants. It has a brilliant golden-yellow crown, crest, and back; blue-edged orange cape; green and black mantle; crimson, purple, black, and brown wings; scarlet underside; and a 6 ft. (1.8 m) long brown and black tracery tail. The female is mainly mottled brown and smaller. There is also a yellow mutation.

The Golden is an excellent beginner's bird, being hardy and adaptable. It mixes well with birds other than gallinaceous species, though there have been occasional losses of chicks of other species. Some females will rear their own chicks, but many will not. In any case, they are easy to rear, and egg production makes up for lost clutches. The Golden will interbreed with Lady Amherst's Pheasant, which has led to a high degree of impurity in the stocks of the latter.

Similar species

Lady Amherst's Pheasant

Ease of care (scale 1–10)

39–47 in. (100–120 cm)

Planted aviary

Heating unnecessary

Keep alone or as pair

Quiet

6–12 eggs

25 days incubation

Ease of care
(scale 1–10)

47 in.
(120 cm)

Planted
aviary

Heating
unnecessary

Keep alone
or as pair

Quiet

6–12 eggs

24 days
incubation

Silver Pheasant

(Lophura nycthemera)

The **Silver Pheasant's** red wattles contrast strikingly with its black and silver coloring.

Native to southern China, Burma, Thailand, and Vietnam, the Silver Pheasant is a striking species. The head and crest, throat, and underparts are black, while the upper parts, including the elegant 24-in. (60-cm) long tail, are white, laced with varying amounts of black. The face has an area of bare red skin. The smaller female is brown with dark striations.

As a wild species, it is probably now extinct in many parts of its range, especially in Vietnam following the war. However, it is well established in aviculture, and popular in spite of its aggressive behavior. Males defending territory will attack almost anything, including you. It is best to have several females with any one male, with plenty of cover for them to hide in.

Females of this free-breeding species will often incubate their own eggs and rear the chicks.

Similar species

Swinhoe's Pheasant

Common Peafowl

(Pavo cristatus)

A listing of pheasant species would hardly be creditable without a mention of the wonderful Indian or Blue Peafowl, with its spectacular colors that defy description. The male's display is chiefly of its huge upper tail coverts, the true tail being virtually hidden and simply used as a support. There are black-shouldered, variegated, and pure white forms, but all are spectacular. The only serious drawback is the birds' raucous calls.

Birds of little brain, peafowl are nevertheless quite fascinating and, if you have the space, they can be allowed to roam at liberty. They have been kept as pets or status symbols for many centuries. They are free breeding, with the hens producing two or three clutches each year. The chicks are quite precocious, being able to fly a short distance as soon as they are dry; but, unlike most other pheasants, they do not pick up their own food for about 10 days. They take live food direct from their mother's beak tip, which makes artificial rearing a demanding process. The long train takes several years to mature, but the young birds will attempt to display from a few days old. Peafowl are hardy and, if free, will roost high in trees.

The full display of a mature male **Peafowl** is quite breathtaking.

Ease of care (scale 1–10) 2

95 in. (200 cm)

Planted aviary

Heating unnecessary

May attack smaller birds

Very noisy

3–6 eggs

28 days incubation

Parrots

A male **Bourke's Parakeet**, originating from southwestern and central Australia. This species is endangered, but recovering well.

Macaws, parrots, cockatoos, cockatiels, parakeets, conures, lories, lorikeets, budgerigars; they are all parrots. No other group of birds is so diverse and yet so similar, recognizable at a glance. Features common to almost all are a large head, smallish eyes, a strong curved beak, and feet with two toes facing forward and two facing back.

Probably more species of parrots have been bred in captivity than any other group of birds. They have been kept as pets since time immemorial. The talking ability of the African Gray is mentioned in the ancient writings of Aristotle and Pliny. Their attractive colors, the ease with which many are tamed and taught to imitate the human voice, and the way they show affection and use their feet as hands combine to make them especially attractive to us.

Parrots vary, from birds which make so much noise as to be deafening – some breeders of large macaws and conures wear ear protectors when tending their collections – to quiet species, like the little Grass Parakeets, which create no problem at all. They range from the rarest birds to the most common bird kept as a pet.

Many species are in desperate trouble in the wild state, and captive breeding programs are established in various parts of the world to try to reverse the situation. Others are regarded as pests. The wild population of Spix's Macaw was recently reduced to one bird, while the Greater Sulfur-Crested Cockatoo is a pest in plague proportions, and its ability to destroy not only crops but even buildings is legendary. In some species the captive population is far more numerous and diverse than the wild one, the New Zealand Kakariki being a case in point. Endangered as a wild species, it is so common in captivity and found in such a number of color mutations that it is one of the few species virtually exempted from the strict control normally placed on rare birds.

In spite of the similarity of their beaks, parrots vary in their feeding habits. Some are brush tongued and feed on nectar; others live largely on fruit; while some, including the large, sad-faced Hyacinth Macaw and the Black Palm Cockatoo, can crush hard nuts that a person has difficulty breaking with a rock.

Most parrots, even nectar feeders and species that eat mostly nuts, may now be fed with commercially prepared feeds. Many breeders have weaned their birds off hard seed and onto pelleted foods which, while they may appear boring to us, have improved the birds' condition, increased the breeding rate, and saved a great deal of waste.

With such power in their beaks, most of the parrot species need to be contained in steel-framed aviaries, or at least double-wired wood frames; otherwise, they simply chew their way out. Where aviaries adjoin, it should be standard practice to use double wire, for parrots' strong beaks can injure other birds, especially their feet. The current trend for breeding these birds is to use all-wire suspended aviaries, which overcome the recurrent problem of parasitic infection through soil-borne bacteria and worms. Yet when viewing parrots kept in such sterile cages and aviaries, I cannot help feeling that these intelligent birds must be desperate for mental stimulation. Even a compatible mate cannot always provide the interest such a bird requires.

Parrots are wonderful, exotic, beautiful, and diverse, and they have to be looked after. All too often one sees solitary birds reduced to feather plucking and self-mutilation. They deserve our admiration and our respect. If we are to keep them in captivity, we should use every means to make sure that they lead full, interesting lives.

A fine example of a male white-winged, violet **Budgerigar**.

Ease of care (scale 1–10) — 4

12 in. (30 cm)

Bare aviary

Heating unnecessary

Keep alone or as pair

Very noisy

2 eggs

24 days incubation

Red Lory

(Eos bornea)

Found in the Moluccan Islands, where it is common in some parts of its range, this is one of the most widely kept and popular of the lory family. It is bright red apart from black primary feathers, and blue wing coverts and undertail coverts. The bill is orange, and the cere (base of the bill) and feet are lead-colored.

Possessed of a strident voice and quite hardy, the Red Lory is best kept in bare outdoor aviaries with a solid floor. Good dry roosting quarters are necessary, although most birds will sleep in their nest boxes. They breed well, with a small clutch, laid on a deep mix of peat and wood shavings. The rearing period is around 2 months.

A mixture of honey, condensed milk, and water, together with multivitamins, may be made up. Alternatively, use a ready-made nectar feed, plus fruit of all kinds, cubed or liquidized. Green food, berries, and small amounts of live food make a good mixed diet, which also produces liquid

This vibrant **Red Lory** looks particularly striking against the green foliage.

droppings – regular cleaning is vital. The birds will also take some small seeds. It is vital to make sure that the nectar mixture does not freeze in cold weather.

Similar species

Black-Capped Lory
Purple-Capped Lory

Ease of care (scale 1–10) — 4

12 in. (30 cm)

Cage

Heating unnecessary

Keep alone or as pair

Very noisy

2 eggs

24 days incubation

Blue Streaked Lory

(Eos reticulata)

This island species was originally found only in the Tanimbar Islands north of northern Australia, but specimens have been introduced into neighboring islands. A red bird with blue and violet streaks on the neck and upper back, with purple feathers that form a band from the eye toward the shoulder, it has a dark orange bill and gray legs and feet.

Increasingly available, the species breeds well and is deservedly popular among aviculturalists. It is hardy and vocal. The chicks are slow to develop for such a relatively small bird, often taking up to 3 months to fledge. Diet and general management are as for the Red Lory.

The **Blue Streaked Lory** is surprisingly hardy, considering its origin.

Dusky Lory
(Pseudos fuscata)

Found in New Guinea and some of the small offshore islands, the Dusky Lory is quite widespread in its range. It is mainly dark brown on the upper surfaces with bands of olive brown and orange yellow, a yellow crown, a yellow collar running between chin and throat, a buff-to-white rump, and an orange bill, so it is not a particularly colorful bird. However, it is active, very intelligent, and very noisy. A good species for the beginner in keeping lories, it is hardy and easily managed, breeding readily and consistently.

In addition to a nectar diet, some mixed canary seeds and millets, soaked seed, and millet spray, together with plenty of fresh chopped fruit and green food, are required.

A typical **Dusky Lory**, perched on a post. This is an intelligent but noisy little bird.

Ease of care (scale 1–10) 4

10 in. (25 cm)

Cage

Heating unnecessary

Keep alone or as pair

Very noisy

2 eggs

24 days incubation

Goldie's Lorikeet
(Trichoglossus goldiei)

This tiny lorikeet is found throughout much of central and Papua New Guinea. A red forehead and crown, mauve ear coverts and cheeks streaked with blue, and a body of green, the lighter underparts streaked with yellow, make this an attractive little bird.

Until recently, the Goldie's was difficult to come by but now, increasingly bred in captivity, it is becoming readily available. It will breed in quite small aviaries or large cages, and is easily managed and surprisingly hardy. Extra light is helpful during long winter nights, and a dry shelter vital. For such a small and inoffensive bird, it is surprisingly and aggressively territorial and needs single accommodations.

A brush-tongued species, they will take some seeds but prefer fruits and nectar. They love sweet grapes and can become very tame when offered such delicacies. Cleanliness is vital for good health, as the Goldie's very liquid and firmly expressed excreta gets everywhere.

Goldie's Lorikeet, a tiny and beautiful nectar feeder, has a great sense of territory.

Similar species

Meyer's Lorikeet

Ease of care (scale 1–10) 4

7 in. (18 cm)

Cage

Heating unnecessary

Keep alone or as pair

Quiet

2 eggs

24 days incubation

2 — Ease of care (scale 1–10)

12 in. (30 cm)

Bare aviary

Heating unnecessary

Keep alone or as pair

Very noisy

2 eggs

26 days incubation

Chattering Lory

(Lorius garrulus)

The **Chattering Lory** is easily recognizable by the flash of green on its wings and thighs.

I t will come as no surprise to learn that this species from the Moluccas lives up to its name. It is not only vocal but colorful, with a scarlet body, green wings and thighs, some yellow on the shoulders and under the wings, and an orange bill.

Widely kept, hardy, and easily managed, the Chattering Lory is a good subject where noise is not a problem. It does best in a single aviary and will become very tame and amusing, spending much time on the wire. Where aviaries adjoin, double wire must be used. Nest boxes are needed for roosting and should be in place all the time.

A diet of nectar and chopped fruits will be readily accepted, along with some soaked seeds and live food.

Similar species

Black-Capped Lory
Purple-Capped Lory

---

8 — Ease of care (scale 1–10)

26–28 in. (65–70 cm)

Bare aviary

Heating unnecessary

Keep alone or as pair

Very noisy

1 eggs

35 days incubation

Palm Cockatoo

(Probosciger aterrimus)

A single **Palm Cockatoo**, looking typically timid despite its size.

T his bizarre-looking bird, all black except for its naked red face, which changes in shade according to its mood and condition, is found in New Guinea, the northern Australian peninsula, and the Aru and Misol islands. It is the largest of the cockatoos. The head and bill are huge, with a long crest of black feathers. The bill is black, and the legs are dark gray. There are three subspecies, of which the Goliath is larger than the Palm.

In spite of its size the bird is gentle, shy, and difficult to maintain. It is very expensive, quite rare, and difficult to breed. One of the hurdles that must be overcome is to find a true pair, for males appear to outnumber females by at least ten to one. If you are lucky enough to obtain a pair, the next hurdle is compatibility.

The bird needs a well-constructed aviary of heavy-duty welded wire with a windbreak as well as a shelter, for it usually roosts in the open. Peanuts, stripped sunflower seeds, unshelled nuts such as almonds and brazils, and plenty of raw vegetables and fruit make a suitable diet.

Rose-Breasted Cockatoo
(Eolophus roseicapillus)

Found across most of Australia, this abundant pink, gray, and white cockatoo, commonly known as the Galah or Roseate, is reproducing in such numbers as to be a serious crop pest. Yet, thanks to the closed door principle of the Australian government on all native wildlife, this once widely kept and popular species is now an expensive rarity. Perhaps in the near future the situation will change and the bird will again become available.

Galahs are being bred, and if you can obtain them, they will usually do very well, being easy to manage and hardy – though also very noisy. A diet of sunflower seeds, pinola, peanuts, vegetables, and pelleted foods gives variety. Breeding pairs need a sturdy aviary, access to nest material in the form of twigs, and a robust nest box, for they are very destructive.

An elegant **Rose-Breasted Cockatoo**, showing off its beautiful breast and head.

Ease of care (scale 1–10) 3

14 in. (36 cm)

Bare aviary

Heating unnecessary

Keep alone or as pair

Very noisy

2–4 eggs

24 days incubation

Greater Sulfur-Crested Cockatoo
(Cacatua galerita)

The **Greater Sulfur-Crest** is probably the best known cockatoo of all.

Largest of the Sulfur-Crested Cockatoos, this species ranges across eastern and south-eastern Australia, and is an introduced species in New Zealand. A large white bird, it has a sulfur-yellow crest with yellow shot through the underside of the wings and tail feathers. The sexes are similar except for eye color, which is dark brown in the male and reddish brown in the female.

Although a pest species, it is extremely popular as an avicultural subject. The species is very long lived – sometimes past 90 – destructive, and noisy. Diet is as for the Rose-Breasted Cockatoo.

Breeding is becoming well established, but the birds can be murderous – especially the smaller Lesser Sulfur-Crested, the male of which not only kills females in sudden attacks of frenzy, but is also savage toward humans when nesting.

Similar species

**Lesser Sulfur-Crested Cockatoo
Triton Cockatoo
Elenora's Cockatoo**

Ease of care (scale 1–10) 2

20 in. (50 cm)

Cage

Heating unnecessary

Keep alone or as pair

Very noisy

2–3 eggs

28 days incubation

Ease of care (scale 1–10) — 2

20 in. (50 cm)

Cage

Heating unnecessary

Keep alone or as pair

Very noisy

2 eggs

28–30 days incubation

Moluccan Cockatoo

(Cacatua moluccensis)

Found in the southern Moluccas, including the islands of Ceram, Saprua, and Haruku, the species is abundant in some parts of its range, but declining. A big, pale pink bird, it has a large and impressive crest of deep pink. The undersides of the wings are suffused with deep pink, and the underside of the tail is shot with pink and orange. It is a shame that so beautiful a bird has a voice that could break glass. The sexes are similar except for eye color, which is as for the Sulfur-Crested.

The Moluccan makes a wonderfully tame and confiding pet if it is hand-reared, and it is in great demand, which makes it expensive. Apart from its loud voice, it is also extremely destructive and will demolish furniture in no time, as it will also destroy any but the strongest cage or aviary.

The popular **Moluccan Cockatoo** can be identified by its pale salmon-pink coloring.

Feeding is as for the Rose-Breasted Cockatoo with a greater range of fruit accepted. Breeding is fraught with difficulties, but breeders are learning their way to increasing success.

Ease of care (scale 1–10) — 2

12 in. (30 cm)

Bare aviary

Heating unnecessary

Keep alone or as pair

Noisy at times

2–3 eggs

28 days incubation

Goffin's Cockatoo

(Cacatua goffini)

Extremely endangered in its wild habitat, the Tanimbar Islands and Indonesia, this small cockatoo is beginning to be bred in increased numbers as breeders establish pairs. It is mainly white with salmon pink between eye and bill, and a suffusion of yellow under the wing and tail. The area around the eye is bare white skin. The sexes are similar except for eye color, as in the Sulfur-Crested.

Hardy, noisy at times, and destructive, they need a strong metal aviary. Unless hand-reared, they do not settle well to cage life. Properly reared birds talk well, and make intelligent and charming, if rather noisy companions.

Diet is as for the Rose-Breasted, but pelleted food is often refused.

Breeding requires a good solid log or a well-reinforced nest box – indeed, that applies equally to all the cockatoos.

A fine example of the white **Goffin's Cockatoo**. This bird makes an intelligent pet.

Cockatiel

(Nymphicus hollandicus)

Ease of care (scale 1–10)

12 in. (30 cm)

Cage

Heating unnecessary

Good mixer

Noisy at times

4–7 eggs

18 days incubation

Hugely popular as a pet, this relatively small bird with a long tail is now available in a considerable and growing number of color mutations. In the original type, the male is smoke gray above, fading to paler gray underneath, darker on the shoulders and underwing coverts. The sides of the face, throat, crest, and forehead are lemon yellow. There is a large orange patch in the middle of the cheeks, a large white wing patch on the coverts, and a dark gray tail, which is black underneath. The female varies in that the yellow areas are smaller and the cheek patches not nearly as bright, the tail is spotted and barred with gray, and the white wing patch is smaller. The chicks on fledging are like the female, but can be identified by their pink cere, which in the adult is black.

As a wild bird, the Cockatiel ranges throughout Australia except for the coastal regions, and can be considered as abundant. The same comment can also be made of the captive birds, which are now bred in such numbers that they are frequently an embarrassment to the breeders. The price of young Cockatiels in the more usual colors is frequently less than the cost of producing them. Responsible breeders now feel that indiscriminate and uncontrolled breeding is irresponsible.

As a cage and aviary bird, it is virtually vice-free, not destructive, and a wonderful mixer with all species – it is almost unheard of for a cockatiel to harm any small bird. Perhaps the only problem is that the cheerful whistling of a few cockatiels can become a nuisance when the group becomes larger.

Unless the bird is kept as a house pet, the best accommodation is an aviary, where it may be safely bred in a colony.

Nest boxes should be fairly large and have a concave base with a little sawdust sprinkled in to keep the eggs together. The clutch is incubated by both parents taking turns. The young should be reared on a mixture of soaked seeds and soft food, various items of green food, and some apple. I find it best to use a commercial soft food rather than mix my own every day.

If you intend to keep these birds as pets, they really need to be hand-reared. In this way they become wonderfully tame and confiding, and learn to talk in a high, squeaky voice. They make pleasant and intelligent house pets.

A male **Cockatiel** resting on a branch in solitary splendor.

Ease of care
(scale 1–10)
4

7¾ in.
(20 cm)

Bare
aviary

Some heat
required

Keep alone
or as pair

Quiet

2–3 eggs

24 days
incubation

Desmarest's Fig Parrot

(Psittaculirostris desmarestii)

This charming little parrot comes from western and southern Papua New Guinea, and islands of the west coast. There are five subspecies with some plumage variation. The nominate race, often called the Golden-Headed Fig Parrot, is green, darker above, with a red forehead, orange-yellow crown and nape, a blue patch in front of the eyes, and a yellow throat with a blue collar above a grass-green breast. The sexes are alike.

Never numerous in aviculture, stocks are building slightly, and this expensive species is beginning to become established. A charming little parrot, it is well worth investing in for the experienced keeper.

Diet must be high in figs – both fresh figs and well-soaked dried figs – with some small seeds, grapes, and other soft fruits, and a little nectar on

Desmarest's Fig Parrot is also known as a "Golden-Headed," for obvious reasons.

occasion. Cleanliness is vital with these soft-feeding birds. Not easy to breed, the Fig Parrot is quite hardy, but needs a nest box throughout the year, with secure and frost-free winter quarters. Extended lighting is helpful.

Ease of care
(scale 1–10)
4

6 in.
(15 cm)

Bare
aviary

Some heat
required

Keep alone
or as pair

Quiet

2 eggs

20 days
incubation

Dwarf Fig Parrot

(Opopsitta diophthalma)

Male and female **Dwarf Fig Parrots** have slight differences in coloring around the face.

Relatively rare in aviculture, the Dwarf Fig Parrot is a small green bird with a scarlet crown and forehead, an orange patch on the back of the head, and a blue stripe from the bill toward the top of the head above the eye. The cheeks and throat are red with a cobalt border below the cheeks. The flanks and sides of the grass-green breast are yellow. The female is similar, but her cheeks are salmon-colored.

Eight subspecies are found throughout New Guinea and the offshore islands, with a population also in northeastern Australia. It is believed to be relatively common.

The bird is not totally hardy and needs care during a hard winter. The species is expensive and seldom available, but very worthwhile if you can obtain it. Breeding is best attempted by using a nest box.

Diet should include seeds, fresh and well-soaked dried figs, and grapes and other soft fruit. Small amounts of nectar may be given.

Grand Eclectus Parrot

(Eclectus r. rotatus)

This is an astonishing parrot, the male and female being so different as to have been thought for many years to be two separate species. The male is brilliant green with a yellow tinge to the head, and blue on the bend of the wing; the outer webs of the primary feathers are mauve, and the underwing coverts red. The sides of the body are red, and the tail is green with the lateral edges blue toward the tip. The underside of the tail is gray with off-white tips. The upper mandible is orange with a yellow tip and the lower is black. The female is mainly bright red with the mantle, lower breast, and abdomen purple. The underwing coverts are dull purple, and there is a mauve line at the bend of the wing. The tail is red above, orange below. The bill is black.

The species is described as common in its native range of New Guinea, the offshore islands, the Moluccas, Aru and Solomon Islands, and northeastern Australia. There are reports of a surplus of males which, considering the colors of the female, is hardly surprising. Few if any are imported today. There are some ten subspecies and one, the Red-Sided Eclectus, which is larger, and in the case of the female a brighter red, is popular in aviculture.

This expensive bird is for the experienced, but once established, it is hardy. It is quite a demanding bird, and needs high-quality food containing Vitamin A. Its diet must consist of a great many fresh vegetables: carrot, corn on the cob, tomatoes, peas, chickweed, dandelion, and so on. Add to this fresh fruit – pomegranates particularly, grapes, and various berries – together with pinola, sunflower seeds, peanuts, hemp, and plain canary seed.

Breeding is now more widespread, but great care must be taken to ensure compatibility. A large

The female **Grand Eclectus** outshines the male with her vibrant coloring.

nest box is desirable and a large aviary, at least 13–16 ft. (4–5 m) long. Chicks leave the nest in 10 or 12 weeks. Many are now hand-reared as pet birds, usually females. This too may have an effect on future breeding programs, as hand-reared birds often either ignore potential mates, or savagely attack them. However, it is not known whether this is true of the Eclectus.

The species can become very confiding, but it is also noisy and destructive.

Similar species

Red-Sided Eclectus

Ease of care (scale 1–10) 5

14 in. (36 cm)

Bare aviary

Heating unnecessary

Keep alone or as pair

Noisy at times

2 eggs

28–30 days incubation

Ease of care (scale 1–10)

16 in. (40 cm)

Bare aviary

Heating unnecessary

Keep alone or as pair

Noisy at times

4–6 eggs

19 days incubation

Barraband Parakeet

(Polytelis swainsonii)

An exclusively Australian species, the Barraband is found in a small area of northern Victoria and New South Wales, where it is relatively abundant.

An elegant bird, it is mainly green with a yellow forehead, cheeks, and throat. A band of red borders the lower throat to the sides of the neck. The outer webs of the primaries are blue, while the tail is green with a black underside. The female lacks the areas of yellow.

Widely kept and popular, the Barraband is hardy and a good breeder. Some birds will not use an artificial nest box and prefer a natural log, but if bred in a colony they may be given a choice.

The species needs space and, being weather resistant, may be housed in long outside flights with access to covered shelters. The adult males may be aggressive toward newly fledged male chicks but, apart from some squabbling, colonies will do very well if they are given room to move. In less spacious surroundings, Barrabands should be restricted to single pairs.

The diet should be mixed canary and millet with sunflower seed, greens, seeding grasses, and some fruit, and also access to gravel.

Similar species

Rock Pebbler

A superb example of the elegant male **Barraband Parakeet**.

Princess of Wales Parakeet

(Polytelis alexandrae)

A rare species in the wild, inhabiting the inhospitable center of Australia, it is now a popular and quite widely kept avicultural species. Light blue on crown and nape, it has upper surfaces of olive green except for a violet rump. The chin, throat, and sides of the neck are pale pink, while the rest of the underside is pale gray-blue with a suffusion of yellow-green. The wings are green, but secondary feathers have a sky-blue suffusion. The long tail is olive with some blue and pink. The female is shorter and has a gray crown, with other colors duller. Lutino and blue mutations have become well established.

A relatively free breeder, it may be bred on the colony system, but all members need to be introduced at the same time or there will be war. Consideration must also be given to this species'

The **Princess of Wales Parakeet** is available in a variety of color mutations.

loud and penetrating call. Diet should consist of canary seeds, millet, sunflower, hemp, green food, and seeding grasses, with gravel to aid digestion.

Ease of care (scale 1–10) 2

18 in. (45 cm)

Bare aviary

Heating unnecessary

Keep alone or as pair

Very noisy

4–6 eggs

19 days incubation

Golden-Mantled Rosella

(Platycercus eximius celiciae)

The species ranges widely throughout south-eastern Australia and Tasmania, is well established as an introduced species in New Zealand, and small feral populations have begun to appear in Britain. This is probably the most widely kept of the larger Australian parakeets.

The head, neck, and upper breast are red, with white cheek patches. The mantle and upper wings are black, with the edges of the feathers yellow. The underwing coverts are blue. The lower breast is yellow, the rump and abdomen are pale green, and the tail is dark green and blue.

Usually free breeding, it often has two clutches in a season. The male is often aggressive, not only with his mate, but with neighbors, so double wire is essential where flights adjoin. A long flight similar to that required by the Barraband is best. Rosellas have a very penetrating call. Diet is as for the Princess of Wales Parakeet, although some pairs will take soft food when rearing chicks. Apple is a favorite, as are blackberries in season.

The various colors of the **Golden-Mantled Rosella** contrast with each other beautifully.

Similar species

Pennant's Parakeet
Stanley Parakeet

Ease of care (scale 1–10) 1

12 in. (30 cm)

Bare aviary

Heating unnecessary

Keep alone or as pair

Noisy at times

3–7 eggs

20 days incubation

Ease of care (scale 1–10)

 10 in. (25 cm)

 Bare aviary

 Heating unnecessary

 Keep alone or as pair

 Quiet

 4–6 eggs

 20 days incubation

Red-Rumped Parakeet

(Psephotus haematonotus)

This excellent beginner's bird is mainly green, brighter on the head and breast, with a blue suffusion on the mantle, yellow underside, and red rump. The tail is blue and green. A yellow mutation is well established.

A long established avicultural species from southeastern Australia, the Red-Rump is easy to manage, hardy, inexpensive, and free-breeding. The males are highly aggressive toward newly fledged males, and should be removed until the chicks can support themselves.

A diet of mixed canary seeds, millet, and sunflower should be supplemented by seeding grasses, apple, and green food.

Similar species

Many-Colored Parakeet

A largely green **Red-Rumped Parakeet**, with the "red rump" clearly visible.

 Ease of care (scale 1–10)

 11 in. (28 cm)

 Bare aviary

 Heating unnecessary

 Keep alone or as pair

 Noisy at times

 3–10 eggs

 20 days incubation

Red-Fronted Kakariki

(Cyanoramphus novaezelandiae)

This **Red-Fronted Kakariki** is endangered in the wild but common in captivity.

The species is declining in its native New Zealand, although some island populations are doing well. This little green parakeet with a red forehead and eye streak and a yellow crown was quite rare in aviculture until the 1970s; since then it has taken off and is now very freely available, with several striking mutations.

A diet of mixed canary seed and millets, with sunflower and green food, should be supplemented with small amounts of live food. Soft food is taken by some birds when rearing young and ignored by others. The species spends a great deal of time on the ground, and many keepers give them chunks of soil with fresh grass to pick through, which also satisfies their liking for some live food.

The Kakariki is multi-brooded if it is allowed to breed throughout the year. This is not recommended for any species, and nest boxes should be removed for the winter and early spring.

Similar species

Yellow-Fronted Kakariki

Splendid Parakeet

(Neophema splendida)

Ease of care (scale 1–10)

7¾ in. (20 cm)

Bare aviary

Heating unnecessary

Good mixer

Quiet

4–6 eggs

18 days incubation

This is the most colorful of the grass parakeets, widely kept and very popular. Most of its plumage is grass-green, with a bright blue forehead, crown, cheeks, chin, and throat, and deep metallic cobalt on the face; the breast is bright red, and the remainder of the underside yellow. The wing coverts are pale blue with the outer webs of the primary feathers dark blue, and the tail is blue-green and yellow. The female is duller and lacks the red breast. There are many mutations available now, most of which are not as splendid and colorful as the original, with the possible exception of the white-breasted blue.

Hailing from the arid interior of southern Australia, the species is not common as a wild bird, no doubt owing to the inhospitable surroundings. It has only recently become numerous in aviculture: 20 years ago it brought a very high price, but now all but the very rarest mutations are relatively inexpensive. Indeed, so varied is the species today that pure-blooded normal birds will soon be in great demand.

The Splendid is a confiding bird and generally very hardy, although it does not like damp conditions. It is free-breeding once settled in, which may take a couple of years, after which time it is difficult to stop. The male birds, like many other parakeets, will not tolerate others of their species, or similar ones, within sight, and will usually show aggression to their male offspring as soon as they are independent.

Otherwise, they are quiet and will mix with unrelated species, even small birds such as canaries, zebra finches, and bengalese.

Diet should include mixed canary seeds and millets, some pinola and sunflower seeds, seeding grasses, and liberal green food. To stimulate breeding, it helps to use a soft food made with a commercial mix folded into a blend of liquified corn, broccoli, and soaked seeds.

When the fledglings leave the nest, they are very nervous and liable to damage themselves by flying into the wire in a panic. A soft mesh drawn tight a few inches below the aviary roof is a help in overcoming the problem, although this still does not stop birds from hitting the sides of the enclosure. It helps to approach the aviary carefully and quietly.

This pair of **Splendid Parakeets** are a blue mutation rather than the usual green.

Ease of care (scale 1–10)

7¾ in. (20 cm)

Bare aviary

Heating unnecessary

Good mixer

Quiet

4–6 eggs

18 days incubation

Bourke's Parakeet

(Neophema bourkii)

Found in the interior of southwestern and central Australia, the species was in serious decline and has been listed as endangered. It is, however, recovering well. Aviculturally, it is in good heart, with a well-established population, including a lovely rose-pink mutation known as the Rosa Bourke's.

The upper parts of the normal bird are brown with lighter margins to the wing coverts. The underside is brown suffused with pink, deeper on the lower breast and abdomen. The forehead, undertail coverts, and sides of the rump are blue, and the wings are edged with violet. The female is paler and shows less blue.

A long established favorite, Bourke's Parakeets are quiet, willing breeders in a 12 × 10 in. (30 × 25 cm) nest box, and usually raise two clutches a year. As with the Splendid, the fledglings are nervous and need particular care. Unusual for a parakeet, the Bourke's is not destructive of plants, although it is easier to maintain a bare flight unless the birds are part of a mixed collection.

Diet and general management are as for the Splendid Parakeet, but with perhaps less reliance on green food.

A beautiful example of a **Bourke's Parakeet** at rest.

Blue-Winged Parakeet

(Neophema chrysostoma)

Not as widely kept as other members of the *Neophema* group, this little parakeet from southeastern Australia and Tasmania is quite abundant over its range. Olive green above, pale green on throat and breast, with yellow underparts, dark blue wing coverts, a blue-gray tail, and a dark blue forehead, this is a colorful bird. The sexes are similar, but the hen is duller.

The Blue-Winged is a charming little bird, totally inoffensive, and may be safely housed with other species. It is hardy and breeds well. The chicks are less nervous on fledging than in other members of the family. General management is similar to the Bourke's Parakeet. This species may also be kept in a planted aviary.

Similar species

Elegant Grass Parakeet

The male **Blue-Winged Parakeet** is more striking than the paler female.

Ease of care (scale 1–10)

7¾ in. (20 cm)

Planted aviary

Heating unnecessary

Good mixer

Quiet

4–6 eggs

18 days incubation

Turquoise Grass Parakeet

(Neophema pulchella)

The bright red flash on the wing marks out this **Turquoise Grass Parakeet** as a male.

Found in southeastern Australia and Victoria, this lovely parakeet is bright green above with a forehead and face of vivid turquoise blue. The upper wing coverts are light blue, and the outer web of the primary feathers a darker blue. The tail is green, and the underside yellow from belly through to the undertail coverts. The male has a red wing band, absent on the female, which is also duller. It has become somewhat uncommon in parts of its range, but is very well established in aviculture, with at least one color mutation and others surely to come.

The Turquoise is a free-breeding species and is easily managed, provided that you follow the rules for all of the other family members – that is, do not mix them, or place more than one pair in any aviary when breeding. The chicks are nervous when fledging, and the males must be watched for aggression toward their male offspring. Pairs should not be housed in adjoining flights.

Feeding and general management are as for the Splendid Parakeet.

Ease of care (scale 1–10)

7¾ in. (20 cm)

Bare aviary

Heating unnecessary

Good mixer

Quiet

4–6 eggs

18 days incubation

A **Lacewing Yellow** with a **Yellow-Winged Green Budgerigar** (above). These young birds will soon show their potential.

The **Spangled Cobalt**, with its blue spangles, is one of the newer color mutations.

Budgerigar

(Melopsittacus undulatus)

The Budgerigar is, without question, the most widely kept caged bird. The species may be divided into two types: the wild type, which is kept simply for pleasure, breeding freely and mostly trouble-free; and the exhibition type, kept by serious breeders, sold for surprising sums, and so large and so coarsely feathered that they have difficulty breeding.

The wild type of Budgie has a yellow forehead, crown, face, chin, and throat; the back, mantle, and wings are yellow brown, and from crown to wings the upper surface is barred with dark brown. The underparts, rump, and tail coverts are bright green, and the long tail feathers are blue. The cheeks have a patch of violet on each side, and there is a necklace of black spots across the throat. The sexes are identical except for the color of their cere, which in the males is bright blue, and in the females is nut brown – however, outside the breeding season the females often have a bluish-white cere. The chicks on leaving the nest have fine bars on the head that cover the forehead, often right to the cere.

There are a great many mutations, the first of which, blue, appears occasionally in the wild, as does the lutino, red-eyed yellow. The basic colors are green, yellow, and blue, with gray, cinnamon,

Ease of care (scale 1–10)

7 in. (18 cm)

Cage

Heating essential

May attack smaller birds

Noisy at times

3–12 eggs

17 days incubation

The **Red-Eyed Lutino** is the albinistic form of the green series.

fallow, etc. Many Budgerigar societies are established throughout the world, some specializing in a particular color variety or form; examples are the Clearwing Society and the Crested Society.

The Budgerigar is free breeding in either cage or bare aviary, although serious breeders of exhibition birds breed all their birds in cages under controlled conditions, pair selection being important to improve the stud. If breeding in an aviary, it is best to establish all the nest boxes at the same height, with more boxes than pairs to avoid squabbling. Some pairs will breed all year round, and it is best to remove the opportunity by either splitting the sexes or removing the boxes during the winter.

The bird is hardy and will withstand even the coldest weather, provided it has access to dry quarters. It mixes reasonably well with birds of similar robustness, and does particularly well with cockatiels and weavers. I have found, however, that they will injure canaries by pulling wings and biting legs, although I always felt it was mischief rather than malice.

Budgerigars do well on a simple diet of plain canary seed and millet, with millet sprays and some green food. They will also rear their chicks without any additions to this diet. However, they must have access to gravel and cuttlefish bone.

The Budgerigar talks very well, although quietly, and many birds have a remarkable repertoire that has been known to exceed 100 words. To teach a bird to talk, it is essential to start with a "bar-head" aged about 6 weeks. Training is by repetition and must include gaining the bird's confidence so that it becomes tame. But while pet Budgies may become very tame, and be allowed their freedom around a house, the moment they go outside they will fly off and be lost.

A light green **English Fallow Budgerigar** with an opaline cinnamon blue Fallow.

This **Budgerigar** is a typical wild specimen from which all captive types derive.

The **Dominant Pied Blue** series (below) is very popular as a show or pet bird.

Ease of care
(scale 1–10)

13 in.
(23 cm)

Bare
aviary

Heating
unnecessary

Keep alone
or as pair

Noisy
at times

3–4 eggs

28 days
incubation

African Grey Parrot

(Psittacus erithacus)

This is the best known and longest established species of parrot kept by humans, in an association dating back at least 2,000 years. It is a West African species, found through the Central African Republic, Kenya, and Angola. It is beginning to decline in some areas, owing partly to commercial trapping and partly to deforestation. Mainly gray with a red tail, it has gray-black primary feathers, and there is a white area of bare skin around the eye. The sexes are identical, but young birds have dark eyes. The feathering of the Grey is tight around the head and neck, giving the bird an almost reptilian appearance at times. It is a very popular pet bird, being an excellent talker once it is tamed. The species is now increasingly being bred, many of the offspring hand-reared as confiding pets – much more so than the nervous, growling wild imported birds.

While the African Grey is a hardy bird and easy to manage, it is less easy to breed than many other species of parrot. Pairs sometimes take years to settle down, and they prefer some seclusion and minimal interference. A strong metal aviary is required, with a hollow log or substantial wooden nest box. A deep layer of wood chippings should be laid inside. It helps to have access to the nest box without going into the aviary, as the birds deeply resent interference.

A varied diet is required with sunflower seed, millets, pinola, peanuts, and lots of fresh vegetables, including corn and broccoli. Fruits such as apple and grapes are also appreciated, and plenty of natural wood, fruitwood preferred, simply to chew to destruction.

Young birds taken as pets need plenty of space, a good large strong cage, frequent interaction with their owner, and a good degree of freedom. If taken outside the confines of the house, they should be wing-clipped to prevent them from flying off. They are highly intelligent birds and, if not given attention, suffer badly from stress and take to feather plucking, which once started is virtually impossible to stop and reduces these beautiful birds to a pitiful state.

A very distinct subspecies of the Grey is the Timneh Grey. Smaller, darker gray, and with a maroon tail, the upper mandible is reddish and tipped with black. Timneh's are now being regularly bred and the young make excellent pets and fine talkers if they are hand-reared.

Similar species

Timneh Grey Parrot

A familiar **African Grey Parrot** showing a glimpse of its unmistakable red tail.

Senegal Parrot

(Poicephalus senegalus)

The **Senegal Parrot** has attractive green back feathers and a gray head.

The *Poicephalus* group of small African parrots has its own specialist society. The Senegal is lead gray on head, face, and nape. The upper parts and a band across the breast are green, the underparts are yellow, and the primaries and tail dark brown. There is an orange-bellied race in Nigeria, Chad, and the Cameroons, and a red-bellied race in Ghana and Nigeria.

There are still considerable numbers of these birds being imported, most of which are male, and none are suitable as cage birds. Senegals are now being bred in increasing numbers, however, and captive-bred hand-reared specimens make charming pet birds. A varied diet should include canary seed and mixed millets, sunflower seeds, millet spray, and seeding grasses, together with fruit, green food, and sprouted seeds.

Similar species

Meyer's Parrot
Brown-Headed Parrot

Ease of care (scale 1–10) 2

9 in. (23 cm)

Bare aviary

Heating unnecessary

Keep alone or as pair

Noisy at times

3–4 eggs

28 days incubation

Peach-Faced Lovebird

(Agapornis roseicollis)

Found in southwestern Africa, this lovebird is mainly green. The forehead, face, chin, throat, and upper breast give it its name, being rose pink. The rump is bright blue, and the tail is green. There are now many attractive mutations.

Usually free-breeding, they do well in a nest box of strong plywood. They prefer strips of willow bark for nest material. Birds will breed throughout the year, but should be restricted to three broods. They are not suitable for colony breeding, as they can be spiteful and quite noisy. Although hardy, they do better if they are given frost-free winter quarters.

Canary seed, millets, spray millet, and seeding grasses should be supplemented with green food, sliced apple, and carrot. High-protein turkey starter and commercial soft foods baked with eggs as a cake will produce large, strong offspring.

Peach-Faced Lovebirds are best kept in pairs if they are to live up to their name.

Similar species

Abyssinian Lovebird
Masked Lovebird
Fischer's Lovebird

Ease of care (scale 1–10) 1

6 in. (15 cm)

Bare aviary

Some heat required

Keep alone or as pair

Noisy at times

3–4 eggs

25 days incubation

Ease of care (scale 1–10)   **5**

 5 in. (13 cm)

 Planted aviary

 Some heat required

 Good mixer

 Quiet

 2–3 eggs

 22 days incubation

Blue-Crowned Hanging Parrot

(Loriculus galgulus)

This tiny and enchanting parrot is found over a wide range of Malaysia, Sumatra, Borneo, and Thailand, with populations in Singapore and outlying islands. It is green with a blue crown, a yellow patch on the nape, bright red throat and rump, and a blue-green tail.

A species that needs some experience, it can be difficult to breed and requires a specialist diet. A secluded planted flight will encourage breeding. Like the lovebirds, it carries nesting material tucked into the body feathers.

The diet should contain a mix of fruit and vegetables, small seeds, figs, and lorikeet liquid nectar. With such a diet, the droppings are very liquid and sticky. The birds roost upside down, often on the aviary or cage wire, ejecting their droppings with force, making cage and aviary wire

A single **Blue-Crowned Hanging Parrot**. This species is diminutive and charming.

cleaning a regular and painstaking affair. Quiet and delicate, they need careful handling, but will reward you with their charming behavior.

Similar species

Vernal Hanging Parrot
Philippines Hanging Parrot

 Ease of care (scale 1–10)   **1**

 22 in. (55 cm)

 Bare aviary

 Heating unnecessary

 Keep alone or as pair

 Very noisy

 2–4 eggs

 28 days incubation

Alexandrine Parakeet

(Psittacula eupatria)

A male **Alexandrine Parakeet** showing off its large and destructive red bill.

A long-established favorite in aviculture, the Alexandrine Parakeet's natural range is from Afghanistan through Pakistan, Burma, Thailand, and Vietnam down to Sri Lanka. The male is largely green, brighter on the forehead, with cheeks and head suffused with gray-blue, a black stripe over the lower cheeks, a pink collar on the nape, a large red patch on the wing coverts, and a long blue tail. The female lacks the black stripe and pink collar. The large red bill gives a clear indication of the bird's destructive powers.

Alexandrines are a free-breeding species, hardy and easily managed. A large, strongly built nest box, at least 30 in. (75 cm) deep, is required; so is a dry shelter that should be frost-free, as these birds are susceptible to frostbite. Diet should include mixed canary seeds and millet, sunflower seeds, plenty of green food, fruit and berries, and lots of fruitwood branches to chew daily. Young birds taken early and hand-reared can make excellent, if somewhat noisy pets, though older birds do not adjust to cage life at all. Youngsters need plenty of freedom and mental stimulation.

Ease of care
(scale 1–10)

16 in.
(40 cm)

Bare
aviary

Heating
unnecessary

Colony
species

Very
noisy

2–6 eggs

24 days
incubation

Indian Ring-Necked Parakeet
(Psittacula krameri manillensis)

Two **Indian Ring-Necked Parakeets**, one a split blue, the other a blue mutation.

This species is abundant throughout its native range of eastern Pakistan, India, Burma, Nepal, and Sri Lanka. Mostly apple green, it has yellowish underparts and a black line from cere to eye; the chin and a stripe across the lower cheeks are also black. The head and nape are pale blue, with a pink collar; the long tail is blue and green. The female lacks the blue and pink areas. There are many lovely color mutations.

Very popular and widely kept, it has been a favorite for many years. Smaller, and therefore slightly less destructive than the Alexandrine, the Ring-Necked is not a suitable bird for cages.

It needs space to move and breed, which may be carried out on the colony system – but be warned that it is rather noisy. Nest boxes need to be substantial and at least 18 in. (45 cm) deep. While quite hardy, the birds must have frost-free quarters as they, like Alexandrines, are susceptible to frostbitten toes. A diet similar to that of the Alexandrine is required.

Similar species

**African Ring-Necked Parakeet
Plum-Headed Parakeet
Mustache Parakeet**

Ease of care
(scale 1–10)

32–34 in.
(80–85 cm)

Bare
aviary

Heating
unnecessary

Keep alone
or as pair

Very
noisy

3–4 eggs

28 days
incubation

Blue and Gold Macaw

(Ara ararauna)

A fine example of the large and popular **Blue and Gold Macaw**.

Found from Panama south through Colombia, the Guianas, Venezuela, Trinidad, Brazil, Bolivia, and Paraguay, this is a widespread species with good populations in many areas, although habitat destruction is having its effect.

Bright blue on its upperparts, it has a green forehead and crown. The cheeks are pinkish with lines of tiny green and black feathers. The underparts are yellow, and the tail is dark blue above, yellow below. The wing primaries are dark blue and the under coverts are sky blue. The sexes are alike, and even behavior is not always a good guide. Surgical or DNA sexing may save a great deal of time if you are attempting to breed this species. One of the most popular macaws, it is now being bred in increasing numbers, which is reflected in falling prices. Wonderful as pet birds, they will also usually stay well at liberty, although they do sometimes fly off.

A very varied diet is most important. Pelleted food should be used as a basis, with a variety of fresh fruit and vegetables – corn on the cob, carrots, peas, broccoli, etc., with pinolas, peanuts, filberts, and brazil nuts, all in their shells. Watching a macaw shell a brazil nut arouses feelings of respect for their power.

When breeding, the Blue and Gold needs a strongly built aviary and an equally strong nest box, a barrel being preferable. Establishing pairs can be tricky, as sometimes birds will fight quite badly. They can be very difficult with people too when breeding, and care is needed. Give them lots of fruitwood to chew, and once the pair has gone to nest make sure that the sitting bird has plenty more to chew inside her barrel; otherwise, she may soon chew her way through the bottom with disastrous results. The chicks are slow to develop, often not leaving the nest for more than 3 months. Unlike many species, the Blue and Gold is not aggressive to its offspring, which may be safely left with the parents for an extended period. Most of the young birds are now being removed for hand rearing, but the parent birds should be allowed to rear at least some of their own chicks.

Similar species

Blue-Throated Macaw

Scarlet Macaw

(Ara macao)

Unrestrained trapping and habitat destruction have made the Scarlet Macaw a declining species over most of its range – Mexico; Central South America, including Colombia, Brazil, Peru, and northern Bolivia; and the island of Trinidad. Fortunately it is now well established as a breeding bird in aviculture. It is mainly scarlet with blue flight feathers. The lower back and upper tail coverts are light blue, and the tail is scarlet with a blue tip. The upper wing coverts are yellow. The bare white face has lines of tiny red feathers. The large bill is white above, black below.

The Scarlet is managed in much the same way as the Blue and Gold, with the proviso that it is, if anything, more aggressive when nesting, and is generally less docile altogether.

The **Scarlet Macaw** is a large and powerful member of the macaw tribe.

Ease of care (scale 1–10)

34–36 in. (85–90 cm)

Bare aviary

Heating unnecessary

Keep alone or as pair

Very noisy

2–4 eggs

28 days incubation

Green-Winged Macaw

(Ara chloroptera)

Like the other large macaws, the Green-Winged is suffering from habitat loss and trapping, but its numbers are reasonable in most areas. Found in Panama, Colombia, Venezuela, Bolivia, Paraguay, Argentina, and the Guianas, it is very widespread. Generally similar to the Scarlet, it has variable amounts of green on the lesser wing coverts. Its large head carries a huge bill, ivory above and black below. The sexes are alike, and surgical sexing is a must if you are to be sure of pairs.

The second largest of the macaw family, in spite of its size the Green-Winged is a gentle giant. A lovely species, it is not so widely kept as the Blue and Gold or Scarlet, but numbers are increasing. Hand-reared birds make the most wonderful and confiding pets. Although vocal, they do not always talk well.

Breeding, diet, and general management are the same as for the Blue and Gold, although as a larger bird it does need more space and certainly plenty of natural wood to chew to bits.

The **Green-Winged Macaw** is a gentle giant in spite of its massive bill.

Ease of care (scale 1–10)

36 in. (90 cm)

Bare aviary

Heating unnecessary

Keep alone or as pair

Very noisy

3–4 eggs

28 days incubation

Ease of care
(scale 1–10)

26 in.
(66 cm)

Bare
aviary

Heating
unnecessary

Keep alone
or as pair

Noisy
at times

4 eggs

28 days
incubation

Military Macaw

(Ara militaris)

The species is found in Mexico, western Colombia, northeastern Ecuador, Peru, and Bolivia. It is a little smaller than the previously described macaws, and has a red forehead, green crown, olive back, blue rump and upper tail coverts, blue and red tail, olive underparts, blue undertail, and flesh-colored face. The sexes are similar.

Not especially popular, the Military Macaw is generally restricted to major collections, although as birds are increasingly bred, more private keepers will be able to obtain them. The Military is very noisy at times and, like most of its relatives, quite destructive.

Diet and general management are similar to that for the Blue and Gold Macaw.

Similar species

Buffon's Macaw

The **Military Macaw** is becoming more popular as captive stocks increase.

Ease of care
(scale 1–10)

19 in.
(48 cm)

Bare
aviary

Heating
unnecessary

Keep alone
or as pair

Noisy
at times

3–4 eggs

26 days
incubation

Red-Bellied Macaw

(Ara manilata)

The Red-Bellied Macaw is found only in southern Colombia and northern and central Brazil. Mainly green, it is darker on the wings, and the center of the belly is maroon, extending toward the vent. The crown is bluish with a tinge of blue on the throat and chest, and the underparts are yellowish.

Like the Military, the Red-Bellied Macaw is relatively rare in aviculture; but, because it is quite a small bird, its popularity should increase as breeding successes make more birds available. It has a pleasant, confiding manner, and can make an excellent pet bird as well as an interesting aviary subject. Diet is as for Hahn's Macaw.

Similar species

Severe Macaw
Yellow-Collared Macaw

The charming **Red-Bellied Macaw** deserves more interest.

Hahn's Macaw

(Ara n. nobilis)

Considerably smaller than the previously described macaws, Hahn's Macaw is found in eastern Venezuela, northeastern Brazil, and the Guianas. Still abundant, its population is being affected by deforestation. Its coloring is dark green with yellowish green underparts, and a blue forehead extending to the crown. The wing has an area of red at the bend, and the underwing coverts are also red. The underside of the primary feathers and tail is yellow. The bill is black, and there is an area of bare white skin on the cheeks.

Never greatly sought after until the price of the larger macaws rose steadily higher, it has now gained in popularity, and is breeding well and therefore available. Because of their small size, Hahn's will no doubt become ever more popular in the future, offering the pleasure of owning a macaw without some of the drawbacks. However, in spite of their small size, Hahn's Macaws need

Hahn's Macaw is ideal for those who lack space but like macaws.

substantial aviaries and sturdy nest boxes. A diet of sunflower and hemp seeds, pinola, peanuts, some canary seed, and maize, together with a pelleted food and a variety of fruits and vegetables, is required, with a high-protein rearing food given before and during the rearing process.

Ease of care (scale 1–10) 3

12–14 in. (30–35 cm)

Bare aviary

Heating unnecessary

Keep alone or as pair

Noisy at times

3–4 eggs

25 days incubation

Sun Conure

(Aratinga solstitialis)

The **Sun Conure** is noisy but nice – a charming little bird.

Never abundant, and thinly spread throughout its range, the Sun Conure is found in northeastern Venezuela, northern Brazil, and the Guianas. Bright yellow above, with a suffusion of orange on the face and breast, this stunning bird has primary feathers of dark blue, a green tail tipped with blue, and wing coverts green tipped with yellow in parts.

Very popular in aviculture, it is hardy and often too free-breeding. Hens can frequently suffer from calcium depletion as a result. Consideration must be given to its loud and discordant voice. It is also very destructive and needs strong accommodations. A diet of sunflower, canary seed, and mixed millets, some hemp, and a variety of fruits and vegetables is recommended.

Similar species

Queen of Bavaria's Conure
Jendava Conure
Nanday Conure

Ease of care (scale 1–10) 1

12 in. (30 cm)

Bare aviary

Heating unnecessary

Keep alone or as pair

Very noisy

3–4 eggs

25 days incubation

Ease of care (scale 1–10) 2

10 in. (25 cm)

Bare aviary

Heating unnecessary

Keep alone or as pair

Noisy at times

4–6 eggs

26 days incubation

Red-Bellied Conure

(Pyrrhura frontalis)

One of the most widely kept of the conures, this bird is popular because it is quieter than species such as the Sun Conure. Found throughout southeastern Brazil, Argentina, Paraguay, and Uraguay, the Red-Bellied is mainly dark green with a band of chestnut on the forehead. The center of the abdomen and a small patch on the back are reddish brown. The throat, neck, and sides of the breast are olive gray. The flight feathers are blue and the tail is green, changing to red toward the tip.

This species is inquisitive, confiding, and easily managed. Many birds become very tame and are reliable breeders. Hardy, they nevertheless need good shelter. Diet should include mixed canary seeds and millets, some pinola and hemp seed, and a good selection of fruits and vegetables. When rearing chicks the birds will take a great deal of

The **Red-Bellied Conure** is a very popular species, confiding and relatively quiet.

soaked seed and high-protein rearing foods, with perhaps some watered-down lorikeet nectar.

Similar species

Mitered Conure
Red-Fronted Conure

Ease of care (scale 1–10) 1

11 in. (28 cm)

Bare aviary

Heating unnecessary

Colony species

Noisy at times

4–7 eggs

28 days incubation

Quaker Parakeet

(Myiopsitta monachus)

The **Quaker Parakeet** is an excellent beginner's bird.

Sometimes called the Monk Parakeet, the Quaker is found in central Bolivia, southern Brazil, and northern Argentina. It has a gray forehead, cheeks, and throat, and gray-brown breast feathers edged with white. The upper surfaces are green, and a broad band of yellow green on the upper abdomen separates these from the brighter yellow of the underparts. The primary feathers are blue, and the tail is green tipped with blue. The Quaker has become virtually domesticated in the United States, and has been banned in some states as wild Quakers (escaped or released birds) have formed flocks that are accused of damaging crops.

Quakers are excellent birds for beginners, but they do have a piercing call. A colony should be allowed to build its own nest, which is a massive structure of twigs, so a good strong aviary with a solid structure on which to base the communal nest is required. Canary seed and mixed millets, hemp seed, sunflower seed, and fruits and vegetables should be supplemented with seeding grasses and soaked seed when the birds are rearing young.

Celestial Parrotlet

(Forpus coelestis)

The **Celestial Parrotlet** needs isolation if you are to succeed.

This dimunitive parrot from western Ecuador and northern Peru is a bright apple green about the head, darker green above and glaucous green below, with lower back, rump, and wing coverts of bright cobalt blue. The female lacks the blue coloration.

Very popular in aviculture, it appears to be coming back to popularity after something of a fall in numbers. It is an easily managed species that breeds well, but is not safe with other species in spite of its small size. The males are quite hard on their mates, which are often stripped bare of feathers about the head and back. They are also noted for their attacks on newly fledged chicks. The Celestial does best in small aviaries, but can be bred in roomy cages.

Canary seed and mixed millets, with spray millet, hemp seed, and green food make a good basic diet, and the birds also need access to seeding grasses and gravel.

Similar species

Yellow-Faced Parrotlet

Ease of care (scale 1–10) 3

5½ in. (14 cm)

Bare aviary

Heating unnecessary

Keep alone or as pair

Quiet

3–8 eggs

18 days incubation

Canary-Winged Parakeet

(Brotogeris versicolurus)

A popular species from eastern Ecuador, Peru, Bolivia, and Brazil, it is dull green with an olive back, and blue-gray around the eyes. The primaries are blue, and the secondaries white with yellow markings. The sexes are alike.

Abundant over much of its range and established as an escaped species in some parts of South America, it is quite hardy and easily managed, but difficult to breed. A strong nest box about 10 in. (25 cm) square is required. Breeding performance may be improved with a high-protein diet, which includes soaked seeds and honey water or lorikeet nectar. At other times, a mixture of canary seed and millet with fruit, green food, and vegetables is adequate. These birds like to roost in their nest box and should be given the opportunity to do so, in frost-free quarters if the weather is severe.

The **Canary-Winged Parakeet** can be difficult to breed but is worth the effort.

Ease of care (scale 1–10) 4

9 in. (23 cm)

Bare aviary

Heating unnecessary

Keep alone or as pair

Noisy at times

3–5 eggs

26 days incubation

Ease of care (scale 1–10) 2

 10 in. (25 cm)

 Bare aviary

 Heating unnecessary

 Keep alone or as pair

 Noisy at times

 3–4 eggs

 26 days incubation

Black-Headed Caique

(Pionites melanocephala)

Colombia, Peru, Venezuela, Brazil, and the Guianas are the home range of this attractive and entertaining parrot. It has a black crown with green around the eyes, and a brownish-green back. The upperparts are green, the throat and undertail yellow. The underparts are yellow-white, and the wings and tail are green. The sexes are alike, and males seem to outnumber females.

The Black-Headed Caique is full of fun and very playful. Hand-reared birds make wonderful pets. It is also an entertaining and interesting aviary bird, and is beginning to breed freely in these conditions.

It thrives on a diet of pinola, sunflower seed, peanuts, hemp seed, millet spray, fruit and vegetables, and plenty of green stuff.

The **Black-Headed Caique** is a most entertaining pet bird.

 Ease of care (scale 1–10) 2

 11 in. (28 cm)

 Bare aviary

 Heating unnecessary

 Keep alone or as pair

 Noisy at times

3–5 eggs

26 days incubation

Blue-Headed Pionus Parrot

(Pionus menstruus)

The **Blue-Headed Pionus Parrot** is a charming little Amazonian.

The regions from Costa Rica south toward the Amazon basin, Bolivia, and Peru are home to this lovely small parrot. It has a blue head, neck, and upper breast, with some red on the throat. Lower down the breast is green with blue edging, and the undertail coverts are red tipped with blue. The upper surface is green with a bronze patch on the shoulders, and the tail is green tipped with blue.

Not yet freely available, the species is a delightful companion bird, quieter than most other Amazon parrots. Breeding is more likely if they are given secluded quarters with plants growing outside rather than inside the flight.

Hardy to some extent, they need frost free-quarters over winter. A diet of canary seed and millet, with sunflower seed, pinola, some peanuts, fruit and vegetables, and sprouted seed is ideal.

Similar species

Dusky Parrot
Red-Billed Parrot
Scaly-Headed Parrot

White-Fronted Amazon Parrot

(Amazona albifrons)

A white forehead and front of the crown give this small Amazon parrot its name. It is mainly green, but blue behind the eyes and face, with red primary and upper tail coverts, yellowish-green vent, and tail green tipped with red. This species has the distinction of being the only Amazon parrot that can be visually sexed, for the female has green wing coverts.

White-Fronteds are quiet in comparison with the other Amazons, and become very tame pets that talk well. They are bred in substantial numbers and therefore are available at rather more affordable prices than many other species. Diet is as for the Blue-Fronted Amazon.

Similar species

Orange-Winged Amazon
Mealy Amazon
Festive Amazon
Green-Cheeked Amazon

Ease of care
(scale 1–10) 2

10 in.
(25 cm)

Bare
aviary

Heating
unnecessary

Keep alone
or as pair

Noisy
at times

4 eggs

24 days
incubation

The **White-Fronted Amazon** is an affordable and charming parrot.

Ease of care (scale 1–10) 2

14 in. (36 cm)

Bare aviary

Heating unnecessary

Keep alone or as pair

Very noisy

3–4 eggs

28 days incubation

Blue-Fronted Amazon Parrot

(Amazona aestiva)

Found in eastern Brazil, with a subspecies *A. a. xanthopteryx* in Bolivia, Paraguay, and Argentina, the Blue-Fronted is often confused with the Orange-Winged Parrot, which also has some blue on the head. Blue-Fronteds are mainly green with an edging of black on the neck and mantle feathers. The forehead has variable amounts of blue, with yellow on the crown and sides of the head and throat. The primaries are tipped with blue, and the outer edges of the secondary feathers are red, as are the shoulders. The bill is black, distinguishing the species from the Orange-Winged, which has a horn-colored bill.

Still abundant in parts of its range, the species is being affected by habitat loss and exports are restricted. It has been a popular cage bird for many years and has also established itself as a breeding species. It is hardy and vocal.

Talented as a talker, the Blue-Fronted needs to be given lots of attention if it is to do well as a pet. Many, sadly, are left to their own devices for most of the day, become bored and feather-pluck, scream for attention, and destroy everything in sight. Prevention is always better than cure, and unless you can give this, or any other large parrot, regular interaction with you or with others of its own species, you should not take it on.

Breeding success would increase if more females were available, for males seem to predominate by quite a large extent. The aviary for any breeding attempt needs to be strong and roomy, at least 15 ft. (4.5 m) long. A barrel nest box should be provided, and access to the nest from outside the aviary is desirable, for males can become extremely savage toward intruders. One advantage of Amazons as breeding birds over African Grays is that you do see rather more of your birds, and if they are talkers, they continue to interact with you.

Peanuts, pinola, sunflower and hemp seed, and corn can be the basis of their diet, with fresh fruit and vegetables, and gravel. Many large parrots also enjoy cooked meat on the bone, which is greatly appreciated. When rearing chicks, bread and milk and soaked seeds, especially sunflower, are taken with relish.

The **Blue-Fronted Amazon** is the best known Amazon parrot, but can be difficult to find.

Double Yellow-Headed Amazon

(Amazona o. tresmariae)

One of three species of Yellow-Headed Amazons, the Double Yellow-Headed is the most spectacular and probably the most sought after. Found as an island species on the Tres Marias Islands, it is mainly green, with variable amounts of yellow on the head, depending on its age. At maturity, its entire head, nape, and part of its back is covered with yellow. The green on back and mantle is edged with black, and the shoulders and outer edges of the secondaries are red. The tail is green with a yellow band.

The species is increasing in popularity, mainly because of its talking ability. Breeding and feeding requirements are similar to those of the Blue-Fronted.

The **Double Yellow-Headed Amazon** is a striking bird and is greatly sought.

Ease of care (scale 1–10) 3

14 in. (36 cm)

Bare aviary

Heating unnecessary

Keep alone or as pair

Very noisy

3–4 eggs

28 days incubation

Hawk-Headed Parrot

(Deroptyrus accipitrinus)

Blue-tipped red feathers on the nape of its neck identify the **Hawk-Headed Parrot**.

Ranging through Venezuela, northern Brazil, Peru, and the Guianas, this species is highly prized and expensive. It is only occasionally imported, and its survival in aviculture rests in the hands of breeders. The Hawk-Headed has a buff-white crown, and the sides of the head are brown with pale streaks. Elongated feathers on the nape are blood red tipped with blue, and are erected to form a spectacular ruff. The breast and abdomen are similarly marked. The upper body surfaces are dark green, the tail is lighter and tipped with blue, and the underside is blue and maroon.

Infrequently bred, the Hawk-Headed needs a secluded aviary as used for birds of prey – that is, with all four sides fully enclosed and only the top wired. Any nest box needs to have access from outside the aviary, with the nest hole capable of being closed off during inspection, for the birds are savagely protective of their eggs and young.

In addition to the usual mix of seeds, nuts, fruit, and vegetables, berries are an important part of their diet.

Ease of care (scale 1–10) 4

14 in. (36 cm)

Bare aviary

Heating unnecessary

Keep alone or as pair

Very noisy

2–3 eggs

26 days incubation

Small Softbills

The distinctive yellow flash of the secondary feathers can clearly be seen on this **Pekin Robin**. This bird is widely available and ideal for the beginner.

Contrary to their name, softbilled birds do not have bills that are soft and rubbery. Indeed, many birds classed as softbills have hard, strong bills. The name is generally used to describe those birds that feed their young directly from the beak tip, rather than with regurgitated food. The term is perhaps better applied to those species that feed on nectar, fruit, and insects – although this, too, is inadequate, as many parrots exist on nectar and fruit, yet are not included in the group. However, in the main, it is a fair description and gives us perhaps the broadest range of all bird types. Those described here range in size from the tiny Indian Zosterop to the impressive Toco Toucan, from the delicate Scarlet-Chested Sunbird to the tough Kookaburra.

Softbilled birds are usually not species for the absolute beginner. A significant number, however, respond well and are easy to care for, some being less delicate than many seed eaters. Many individuals become tame and confiding, which is an added pleasure. Most often, the governing criteria is space. Many need spacious single accommodation, well planted and often heated in winter, and as such are beyond the reach of the small aviculturalist.

They also fall into two categories as far as their legal requirements are concerned. European species, with a very few exceptions, need to have proof of captive breeding before they may be traded, and most are not allowed to be exhibited without special exemption licenses. Proof of captive breeding generally means that the birds

The classic **Toco Toucan** with its unmistakable enormous yellow bill. It is rare in aviculture as it requires expertise and space.

must have appropriate-sized closed metal rings, although in time DNA testing may be used instead. Already microchip implants provide an infallible guide to recognition, although they do not prove breeding. Non-European species, apart from a few that are restricted by CITES, are often freely available.

Success with softbills invariably means dealing with live food. Wriggling mealworms, squashy wax moth larvae, crickets that escape to hide and chirrup but remain out of reach, and dead baby rats and mice (known disarmingly as "pinkies") which must be kept in the freezer until required, are not to everyone's taste.

When attempting to breed any species, you are more likely to succeed if you plan ahead. With softbills, such plans include a production line for live food. Small insectivorous chicks remain in the nest for 2 or 3 weeks only, but during this time they consume vast amounts of live food. In two months, one brood of medium-sized softbills ate 11 lb. (5 kg) of mealworms, 6½ lb. (3 kg) of crickets, and two large ox hearts of about 5½ lb. (2 kg) each. Each bird weighed around 5¼ oz. (150 g) when fully grown.

Fruitfly cultures need to be established in advance to provide a continuous supply. Wax moth larvae, which are frighteningly expensive and sold by number only, keep for about two weeks. Crickets and locusts can be slowed down in the refrigerator. Housefly larvae can be produced easily enough, but must be thoroughly cleaned and are better used in their inert pupal stage, or as hatchling flies. With winged flies, it helps to put the unhatched pupae in a glass jar with a cover that has one escape hole, so that they are released slowly.

The average backyard is an invaluable source of fresh and varied live food, but should be used only if you do not use pesticides. Shake shrubs and bushes into an upturned umbrella to extract small insects and spiders.

Softbills very often need specialist feeding. There are recipes for making insectivore mixtures, nectar, and so on, but there are always worries that homemade mixtures may not be easily repeatable, turn sour, or be missing vital trace elements. It is much safer to stick to an established brand of the required diet. There are now nutritionally balanced diets for almost all birds, including some with a probiotic ingredient to stimulate reluctant appetites and adjust gut flora.

When it comes to fruit, a general rule of thumb should be "If it is not suitable for you, then it is not suitable for your birds." There is little point in buying delicate and expensive birds, only to lose them through feeding sub-standard food. Today there are really very few fruits that are unavailable out of season, and apples, pears, grapes, sweet oranges, and tomatoes can be bought throughout the year. Bananas are better used as a base for fruitfly cultures than fed to birds. Some species need diced fruit; others will feed from halves which, while wasteful at times, may be the only way in which the particular species is willing or able to take the food. At least you can use the remains to establish another fruitfly culture.

Berries are a different story. If you have species that enjoy berries, the autumn surfeit of blackberries, blueberries, and elder, hawthorn, rowan, and pyracantha berries should be picked at their best and frozen. Some berries, such as hawthorn, appear not to be palatable until they have been frosted. Often wild birds have stripped the clusters, as is their right, leaving few for your birds, so picking early and freezing serves two purposes. Note, though, that even if wild birds have been eating berries, it does not mean that they are suitable for your birds, so take care with what you harvest.

Aviary design is important, and particular attention needs to be given to adequate winter quarters. In temperate climates, winters are generally too cold for most exotic species to be left outside unprotected. Provision needs to be made for enclosing delicate birds, and installing lighting and heating. Not only must temperatures be maintained, but day length may also need to be adjusted to allow birds with a high metabolic rate enough time to feed.

When planting aviaries, take care with the choice of plants. It may be to your temporary advantage to have rampant growth to give instant cover, but some plants can take over all the interior space in no time and mean you will be constantly

A blue-winged **Kookaburra**, originating from Australia and Tasmania. This bird has a well-known laughing call.

cutting back in order to see your birds and give them room to move. Russian vine is a notorious example. If space is critical, use annual climbing plants, such as hops or string beans. These two will bring small insects into the aviary, which add interest to the diet of your birds without making a takeover bid.

Most of the softbilled birds referred to in this chapter are usually obtained as imported exotics. If we wish to continue keeping these birds, then it falls upon us to build our captive stocks. Pekin Robins are imported in large numbers, but not bred nearly as often as they should be. Scarlet Tanagers, found only in Brazil, are probably no longer in any collections, as the Brazilian border has been closed to wildlife export since 1967. Meanwhile, their habitat is rapidly being destroyed. Unless we establish breeding populations of even the most common species, one day those birds may become merely a memory.

Ease of care (scale 1–10) — 2

13 in. (33 cm)

Planted aviary

Some heat required

May attack small birds

Noisy at times

2–4 eggs

14 days incubation

Red-Faced Mousebird

(Colius indicus)

Named after their behavior rather than their diet, Red-Faced Mousebirds creep through vegetation like mice. They are also rather mouse-colored, being almost entirely gray-green except for the bare skin around the face, which is red. The dark brown feet, armed with strong claws, are unusual in that all four toes can be turned forward, by which adaptation these birds usually sleep clinging to a tree trunk, head upward.

Found in southern Tanzania, south to Malawi, and southern Africa, they are fruit eaters and are destroyed as a crop pest. An interesting and easily managed species, they fare best in small groups. They are not found in many collections, but are a worthwhile inclusion.

Given plenty of vegetation cover, Mousebirds are free breeding, building a cup nest on a platform of twigs. They are not hardy and need a heated enclosure during severe weather. The birds

The secretive **Red-Faced Mousebird** is named for its behavior.

should be encouraged to sleep inside a shelter, as they tend to sleep hanging on the wire, which leaves them easy prey for night predators. In addition to a diet of fruit and insectivore mixture, they take small live food such as crickets and mealworms, and may also take pinkie mice, as they are known to steal nestling birds.

Ease of care (scale 1–10) — 5

16 in. (40 cm)

Planted aviary

Heating unnecessary

Keep alone or as pair

Noisy at times

2 eggs

20 days incubation

Hartlaub's Touraco

(Tauraco hartlaub)

Hartlaub's Touraco is spectacular, active, and entertaining.

Kenya and northern Tanzania are home to this spectacular and colorful bird. The crown, crest, and sides of the head are glossy blue, and the throat, ear coverts, mantle, neck, and breast glossy green. The tail and rump are violet, and the wings are a similar color with bright red primary feathers. The abdomen and undertail are blackish. There is a conspicuous white spot in front of the eye and a fine white line below the eye. The sexes are alike.

This active, bouncy species gives hours of entertainment, and it is essential to give it plenty of space. The diet is diced fruits and berries, with some commercial insectivorous mixture, soaked trout pellets, and live food when the birds are rearing chicks. Reasonably hardy, they need dry accommodations over winter, but can usually get by without any heat, except in extreme conditions.

Similar species

Livingstone's Touraco

White-Cheeked Touraco

(Tauraco leucotis)

The **White-Cheeked Touraco** is widely kept and deservedly popular.

A native of Ethiopia and southeastern Sudan, the active White-Cheeked Touraco is regularly seen in aviculture. The head, neck, mantle, back, and breast are green; wing coverts and rump blue-gray; primary feathers red; and tail blue. White patches on the cheeks and in front of the eye give the species its name. The whole is topped off with a short dark blue crest. The sexes are alike.

A willing breeder, the White-Cheeked Touraco is the most widely kept of the genus and is very popular. It needs space and height, with plenty of large natural perches along which it can run and bounce. A wire netting foundation placed in cover, with the basis of a twig nest wired into place, will encourage it to breed.

The species is not altogether hardy, and roomy frost-free quarters should be provided in winter. Diet should consist of diced fruits – apple, pear, tomato, etc. – with a commercial insectivore food and berries in season. Live food is usually ignored, even when the birds are rearing chicks, which they feed on regurgitated fruit.

Ease of care (scale 1–10) 5

16 in. (40 cm)

Planted aviary

Some heat required

Keep alone or as pair

Noisy at times

2 eggs

20 days incubation

Kookaburra

(Dacelo novaeguineae)

The **Kookaburra** is famous for its loud, hysterical laughing call.

Found only in Australia and Tasmania, this bird is brown on the back and wings, with prominent blue spots on the shoulder, a brown eye stripe, and a barred black and rufous tail with a white tip, creamy white undersides, head, and neck, and a large bill like that of a kingfisher.

If you can obtain a true pair (the sexes are alike), breeding is only a matter of time, for the Kookaburra is proving quite prolific. A long rectangular nest box, set at a 30° angle to form a tunnel with the nest chamber, or a hollow log set at a similar angle, will encourage breeding.

A diet of dead mice and rats, dead day-old chicks, and diced meat is the basic requirement. Very often, only one chick from a clutch survives, and it may be best to hand-rear any offspring, which should be fed a ground-up version of the adult diet, without skin or feathers for the first few days.

Roomy accommodations are needed, with shelter from cold and wet weather. The birds' well-known hysterical laughing call may seriously annoy your neighbors.

Ease of care (scale 1–10) 3

18 in. (45 cm)

Bare aviary

Heating unnecessary

Keep alone or as pair

Very noisy

2–4 eggs

25 days incubation

Ease of care
(scale 1–10)

3

18 in.
(45 cm)

Planted
aviary

Some heat
required

Keep alone
or as pair

Noisy
at times

2–3 eggs

21 days
incubation

Blue-Crowned Motmot

(Momotus momota)

There are 22 described subspecies of this bird, found extensively throughout much of South America from Mexico to Argentina. The forehead and sides of the head are iridescent turquoise blue below a black crown. A black eye stripe starts at the base of the forehead, and the black of the bill extends through the eye like a bandit mask. The body and wings are green, and there is a black spot in the center of the breast. The long green and blue tail has bare subterminal shafts, each with a dark tip.

At one time this was a very popular species in larger collections, but now it is less frequently seen. With deforestation destroying so much of their habitat, it would be wise to build numbers of the Motmot in aviculture.

As tunnel-nesting species, Motmots may be difficult to cater for, but a peat bale will give a good basis for nest building. A tropical house environment is best since they are not hardy, although they will do well in outside aviaries during summer months in temperate climates. Cold nights are not at all to their liking.

They are often fed on fruit, but this is not a suitable diet, and a good insectivore mix should be given as a small proportion of a mainly live-food diet of crickets, mealworms, locusts, pinkie mice, and ground beef. Motmots are not safe with small birds, which they may eat.

The **Blue-Crowned Motmot** needs attention if it is to be maintained in aviculture.

Red-Headed Barbet

(Eubucco bourcierii)

This brilliant species is found in Colombia, Costa Rica, Ecuador, and Panama. In the male the whole of the head, throat, and upper breast are scarlet; the back is green with a line of pale blue on the neck; the underparts are orange fading to yellow; and there are green and white streaks on the flanks. The female has blue cheeks, a gray throat, a yellow band across the breast, and a black and gold crown, making her even more colorful than the splendid male.

Probably the most popular of the barbets, it is only occasionally available. It is delicate, needing dry, warm conditions in winter. Highly insectivorous, it requires live food in quantity, particularly when breeding, together with an insectivore mixture, fruit, and berries in season. Barbets are hole nesters and will use either a nest box or a hollow log, with the parents sharing incubation.

The **Red-Headed Barbet** is an interesting middle-sized softbill.

Similar species

Blue-Throated Barbet
D'Arnaud's Barbet
Black-Collared Barbet

Ease of care (scale 1–10) 3

6¾ in. (17 cm)

Planted aviary

Some heat required

Good mixer

Quiet

2–4 eggs

14 days incubation

Red-Billed Hornbill

(Tockus erythrorhynchus)

Abundant in many of the drier areas of northern and central Africa, the Red-Billed Hornbill is a black and gray bird with white spotting on the wings, a white strip above the eye, and a long tail with black central feathers and black and white outers. The long curved bill is bright red. The sexes are similar, although the male has a black base to the lower mandible that may not be present in the female. This species is fascinating, but is not suitable for beginners.

Red-Billed Hornbills are hardy once established, but they should not be allowed access to outside aviaries in frosty weather for fear of damage to their delicate feet. Relatively free breeding, they need a deep log and access to mud for, as with all hornbill species, the female is walled in by her mate during the 3 months of incubation and rearing. A basic diet of a commercial insectivore food should be supplemented by diced meat, diced fruit, and berries. Successful rearing calls for live food: mealworms, locusts, crickets, pinkie mice, and larger dead mice and rats.

Similar species

Yellow-Billed Hornbill
Von der Decken's Hornbill

The **Red-Billed Hornbill** is not easy to keep, but is worth the effort.

Ease of care (scale 1–10) 6

17½ in. (44 cm)

Planted aviary

Some heat required

May attack smaller birds

Noisy at times

3–6 eggs

30 days incubation

3 Ease of care
(scale 1–10)

10¼ in.
(26 cm)

Planted
aviary

Some heat
required

Keep alone
or as pair

Quiet

2–3 eggs

21 days
incubation

Lettered Aracari

(Pteroglossus inscriptus)

Found only in central and southern areas of Brazil, the Lettered Aracari is dark green above and lighter green below, turning yellowish toward the abdomen, with chestnut on the thighs and rather brighter red on the rump, and a glossy black head. The upper mandible is whitish buff, with a black ridge and a black tip, and black lines running vertically along its length. The lower mandible is black. The female is similar except for a chestnut head.

Now quite rarely available, this was once a very popular avicultural species. It is best suited to large indoor accommodations, and may be induced to breed in a nest box or large hollow log. The young of one year will frequently assist in the rearing of the subsequent year's brood. Diet should be based on mixed diced fruits, berries, and

The **Lettered Aracari** is a good introduction to toucans.

insectivorous mixture, with plenty of live food – especially during the rearing of chicks, when insects will be eaten almost exclusively for the first 10 days or so.

6 Ease of care
(scale 1–10)

22 in.
(55 cm)

Planted
aviary

Some heat
required

Keep alone
or as pair

Quiet

2–4 eggs

17 days
incubation

Toco Toucan

(Ramphastros toco)

The huge bill of the **Toco Toucan** surprisingly weighs almost nothing.

When anyone thinks of a toucan, this is the bird that comes to mind. Found in a wide area across South America from Brazil to Argentina, it is glossy black with a white throat, breast, and rump, and a blue ring around the eye. Its huge but lightweight bill is bright golden orange with a black base and a black oval at the tip. The sexes are alike.

Rare in aviculture but still available occasionally, the Toco requires expertise and a great deal of space, which also includes height. Substantial indoor quarters are required during cold weather as small enclosures do not suit Tocos. Captive breeding is uncommon. The diet should be based on a good mixture of fruit and insectivorous mixture, the fruit diced large enough for the bird to pick up, together with large crickets, locusts, giant mealworms, and dead mice or rat pups.

Similar species

**Channel-Billed Toucan
Sulfur-Breasted Toucan
Swainson's Toucan**

Ease of care
(scale 1–10)

7 ¾ in.
(20 cm)

Planted
aviary

Some heat
required

Keep alone
or as pair

Quiet

2–4 eggs

14 days
incubation

Golden-Fronted Fruitsucker

(Chloropsis aurifrons)

The **Golden-Fronted Fruitsucker** becomes very tame and is a wonderful mimic.

Found in much of India and the dense forests to the east, this species, also known as the Golden-Fronted Leafbird, is bright green with a golden forehead, a black face, chin, and throat bordered with yellow, a metallic blue mustachial streak, and turquoise blue on the bend of the wing. The long scimitar beak is black. The female and immature males are paler.

The best-known avicultural member of its family, the Golden-Fronted is delicate until established, after which it will live a long time, well over 20 years. The bird is an accomplished mimic of other birds' song, often singing from dawn to dusk. Single birds kept as pets will become finger tame in no time, responding to live food, mealworms usually, although these should be restricted to no more than 10 a day.

The usual recommended diet is a mixture of fruit and insectivorous mixture, but these birds also enjoy nectar. Fresh orange juice is also a great favorite. If oranges are given in halves, the bird sucks the juice and gets very sticky in the process, so juice given in a drinker saves a great deal of mess. If caged, the bird must be given ample opportunity for bathing. A deep layer of newspaper on the cage bottom, replaced daily, will help keep it in good feather condition.

Breeding has been achieved, although infrequently. It is essential to make sure the pair is compatible by means of staged introductions. Rearing success depends on as much live food as possible, using caterpillars, spiders, and small grubs rather than mealworms.

Similar species

Hardwick's Fruitsucker
Blue-Winged Fruitsucker

 Ease of care (scale 1–10) — 2

 7¾ in. (20 cm)

 Planted aviary

 Heating unnecessary

 Keep alone or as pair

 Quiet

 3–4 eggs

 14 days incubation

Red-Whiskered Bulbul

(Pycnonotus jocusus)

Of all the many Bulbuls, there being some 48 *Pycnonotus* species and over 200 subspecies, the Red-Whiskered is the best known in aviculture and very popular. Found in India, Burma, Thailand, Vietnam, and China, it is a brown bird with a dark brown crest, a white cheek patch, and a red tuft extending behind the eye. The underparts are white with a buff area on the flanks.

Though far from colorful, Red-Whiskered Bulbuls are a good beginner's species, active and confiding, easy to care for, hardy, long-lived, and melodious. If you can obtain a true pair – for the sexes are alike – they can be very free breeding. They are reasonable mixers: single birds are best in company, but pairs must be isolated if they show signs of nesting, for they become very aggressive at this time. They need plenty of cover and a choice of nest sites. Moss is the basis for the nest, and fine grasses are used for the lining. Diet

The **Red-Whiskered Bulbul** makes a good breeding bird and can become very tame.

is fruits and insectivorous mixture, with small live food when rearing chicks.

Similar species

Red-Vented Bulbul
Red-Eyed Bulbul
Chinese Bulbul

 Ease of care (scale 1–10) — 3

 10 in. (25 cm)

 Planted aviary

 Some heat required

 Keep alone or as pair

 Noisy at times

 2 eggs

 14 days incubation

Fairy Bluebird

(Irena puella)

Widespread through much of India, Burma, Malaysia, Thailand, and Borneo, this species is a spectacular shining light blue on the top of the head, with the color running down the nape across the shoulders and mantle over the back rump and tail coverts, while the rest of the plumage is black.

Once almost impossible to obtain, this is very much a favorite softbill species today. It is easy to manage, but needs space. The birds are fairly willing breeders, needing their own accommodations, where they will build a flimsy nest in cover. An open-fronted box or a suitable-sized wicker nest basket will encourage them.

Diet is a mixture of diced fruit and insectivorous mixture, with regular supplies of live food, which are particularly important when the birds are feeding chicks.

The **Fairy Bluebird** is a brilliant electric blue, which flashes in the sunlight.

Cedar Waxwing

(Bombycilla cedrorum)

The Cedar Waxwing is found in North and South America, from Canada to Colombia. It is olive brown, paler underneath, with a crest that is rarely raised, a black mask from the base of the beak through the eye, and a dark, yellow-tipped tail. The secondary feathers have red waxy tips. It was thought at one time that the number of tips indicated sex, but that appears not to be so.

They are easily managed though difficult to breed. A colony system appears to improve the chances. Plenty of cover is required, and lots of live food. Bluebottle flies, slowly released from a hatchling jar with a hole in the top, attract the birds, and ant eggs and wax moth larvae are also taken in small quantities. The diet otherwise is a good insectivore mixture with lots of apple, raisins, and berries. Waxwings will take rowan, pyracantha, and blackberries with relish, and a frozen stock will aid you throughout the year.

Ripe berries are a favorite food for the lovely **Cedar Waxwing**.

Similar species

Bohemian Waxwing
Japanese Waxwing

 Ease of care (scale 1–10) 4
 6 in. (15 cm)
 Planted aviary
 Heating unnecessary
 Keep alone or as pair
 Quiet
 4–5 eggs
 14 days incubation

Dunnock

(Prunela modularis)

Few British gardens are complete without this secretive but confiding little bird, found throughout Europe and east as far as Iran. It is slate gray and brown striped, with more brown above and more slate below, an indistinct wing bar, and a dark brown bill. This rather drab coloring is compensated for by a cheerful if repetitive little song.

Best kept in an outside flight with plenty of vegetation and ground cover, the bird will breed quite well, making a neat cup of fine roots and grasses inside a rough exterior of twigs. It is hardy and may be left outside throughout the year provided it has access to a dry roost.

Diet is an insectivorous mixture and seeds – a good canary mix plus some wild seeds. Live food is required when rearing young.

The **Dunnock** is common and quiet, with a sweet song.

 Ease of care (scale 1–10) 2
5½ in. (14 cm)
Planted aviary
Heating unnecessary
Good mixer
Quiet
 4 eggs
 12 days incubation

Ease of care
(scale 1–10)

 5½ in.
(14 cm)

 Planted
aviary

 Heating
unnecessary

 Keep alone
or as pair

 Quiet

 4–5 eggs

 14 days
incubation

Siberian Rubythroat

(Erithacus calliope)

Found in Siberia and wintering in India and southern China, the Rubythroat is a small olive-brown thrush with a prominent eye stripe and mustachial streak. The chin and throat are bright red with a gray border. Underparts are gray brown, fading to gray-white on the abdomen. The paler female lacks the red throat.

There appear to be good populations in many parts of the range, but in some places, birds are rarely available and highly sought. Not compatible with other species, they are also difficult to keep in pairs, and should be housed separately outside the breeding season. They are hardy and will winter outside in all but the worst conditions.

Diet should consist of a good small insectivore mixture with ant eggs and other small live foods, such as tiny crickets and wax moth larvae, with anything collected from the wild, such as small caterpillars and spiders.

The **Siberian Rubythroat** needs peace and isolation to breed.

 Ease of care
(scale 1–10)

 7¾ in.
(20 cm)

 Planted
aviary

 Some heat
required

 May attack
smaller birds

 Quiet

 2–3 eggs

14 days
incubation

Snow-Headed Robin Chat

(Cossyphla niveicapilla)

Widespread across Africa from Senegal to Sudan and south to Uganda and Kenya, the Robin Chat has a white forehead and crown, dark slate-gray wings and mantle, neck and undersides of orange-red, and a black and orange tail.

Excellent avicultural specimens in an aviary that can be heated in winter, they are becoming available more often, and breeding has been recorded. They will even tolerate other species while doing so, provided that these are not close relatives. It is better to give them single accommodations, however.

The stable diet is a good insectivore mixture with live food in the form of small locusts and crickets and a few mealworms. Some birds will take a little fruit.

The **Snowy-Headed Robin Chat** is a lovely species for the experienced keeper.

White-Rumped Shama

(Copsychus malabaricus)

Usually described as an Indian bird, in fact it ranges across most of Asia with 18 subspecies. It is glossy black with chestnut underparts, a white rump, and a long black and white graduated tail. The female is gray rather than black and has a shorter tail.

This bird is highly rated as an avicultural specimen, but it is delicate and sometimes difficult to establish, and also is not available in any numbers. It has a melodic and infinitely variable song, much of which is mimicry. It is considered to be the most fluid singer of all exotic species.

Most Shamas now appear to be kept as single pets. This is sad, as any such delicate species should be bred to improve its avicultural standing wherever possible. Breeding is not easy, as pairs need to be housed apart outside the breeding season; they often fight during it. They also need copious and varied live food even to contemplate breeding, and vast amounts when rearing chicks.

The **White-Rumped Shama** is a delicate, wonderful songster – the Indian Nightingale.

A diet of good insectivore mixture must be supplemented with abundant live food. Blowfly larvae may be used to encourage newly imported birds to start eating foods they are not used to.

 Ease of care (scale 1–10) 7

 11 in. (28 cm)

 Planted aviary

 Some heat required

 Keep alone or as pair

 Quiet

 4–5 eggs

 14 days incubation

White-Capped Redstart

(Phoenicurus leucocephalus)

Found mainly in the Himalayas, northern Burma, and Indochina, this species is marked in a similar fashion to the Shama, black above and chestnut below, but with a white crown and nape, a chestnut rump, and a tail ending in a black band. The sexes are alike.

Occasionally available, this is a bird for experienced keepers and needs abundant, very small live food: bloodworms, fruit flies and their larvae, small spiders, and caterpillars. Breeding is possible given abundant live food, dense cover, and running water; these birds love a waterside environment. Once they have been established, they are quite hardy and will live outside with a frost-free shelter.

The **White-Capped Redstart** is not often available but highly sought.

 Ease of care (scale 1–10) 6

 6¼ in. (16 cm)

 Planted aviary

 Heating unnecessary

 Keep alone or as pair

 Quiet

 3–4 eggs

 14 days incubation

2 Ease of care (scale 1–10)

10 in. (25 cm)

Planted aviary

Heating unnecessary

Keep alone or as pair

Noisy at times

3–6 eggs

14 days incubation

European Blackbird

(Turdus merula)

An amazingly widespread species, it is found in 16 subspecies throughout Europe, North Africa, the Middle East, Central Asia, India, Pakistan, and southern China, and it has been introduced into New Zealand. Males are all black with a yellow bill, females brown, darker above, with a pale brown bill. Immatures are similar to the female, but spotted on the brown breast. This species is now available in a number of mutations including white, cinnamon, cream, and pied. Albino and partially albino birds occur naturally.

The blackbird is a willing breeder in aviculture, but must be established with care to avoid fighting. Nests are usually made in open-fronted wooden boxes tucked into cover, and are made of grasses, rootlets, and various plant fibers. Wet mud is also required to hold the nest together.

The **European Blackbird** is found in a series of color mutations as well as jet black.

Fruit, vegetables including cooked potatoes, peas, and corn, and soaked puppy meal should be added to a good large insectivore mixture. Blackbirds love berries in season and will do anything for strawberries.

The song is well known and carries far. It is often used today as an example of background sound when fighting complaints of bird noise, since it is one of the loudest songs of any European bird. The power of a blackbird can only be appreciated when a male sings inside a small room, when it is probably above industrial safety levels. An established pair can be amazingly productive, producing three or more clutches of chicks in a year if allowed.

Similar species

Song Thrush
Mistle Thrush
Dusky Thrush
Chestnut-Capped Thrush
Olive Thrush

White-Crested Laughing Thrush

(Garrulux albogularis)

The **White-Crested** is the most readily available of all the many laughing thrushes.

This large thrush is found in Pakistan, northern India, the Himalayas, and as far east as Vietnam. The white of the upper breast, throat, and all of the head and crest is set off by a black stripe through the eye, while the remainder is olive and rufous brown. The sexes are similar.

The species is hardy, easily available, and easily managed, but requires lots of room for it is very active. Breeding is more frequent now that a wide range of live food is easy to obtain. Without massive amounts of live food, any chicks will be eaten by their parents.

A good large insectivore mixture should be supplemented by raw ground meat – ox heart is ideal – live food, and the occasional dead mouse. Laughing Thrushes will live in small groups.

Similar species

White-Throated Laughing Thrush
Red-Capped Laughing Thrush
Black-Throated Laughing Thrush
Green-Winged Laughing Thrush

Ease of care (scale 1–10) 2

12 in. (30 cm)

Planted aviary

Heating unnecessary

Colony species

Noisy at times

3–4 eggs

14 days incubation

Silver-Eared Mesia

(Leiothrix argentauris)

With seven described subspecies, the Silver-Eared Mesia inhabits a large area of India, Burma, Thailand, Indochina, and Malaysia. The upper parts are brown with an orange forehead, chin, and throat. The crown and the sides of the face are black, and there are large silver patches behind the eyes. The tail coverts and rump are red, with red and orange wing coverts. The underparts are buff. The female is less bright, and the rump and tail coverts are orange to buff.

Birds are available in variable quantities. They are likely to breed if given good cover to match their secretive behavior. A diet of diced fruit and a good insectivore mixture should be improved with live food in quantity once breeding begins.

A reasonable songster, the Silver-Eared mixes well with birds of similar size outside the breeding season, but is an accomplished nest robber if given the chance.

The **Silver-Eared Mesia** is a good species with which to start keeping softbills.

Ease of care (scale 1–10) 2

7 in. (18 cm)

Planted aviary

Heating unnecessary

May attack smaller birds

Quiet

3–4 eggs

14 days incubation

Ease of care (scale 1–10)

6 in. (15 cm)

Planted aviary

Heating unnecessary

May attack smaller birds

Quiet

3–4 eggs

14 days incubation

Pekin Robin

(Leothrix lutea)

The most widely available and popular softbill, this is the perfect bird for the beginner moving up from seed eaters. It is common in India and Burma through to Vietnam and southern China, and has been introduced into Hawaii. Olive gray on the back and wings with a yellow flash on the secondaries, it has a bright olive head and nape. The chin and throat are yellow with an orange edge, the underparts yellow with gray flanks and a gray mustachial stripe. The darker tail has two white crescent moon marks halfway down its length. The sexes are similar: hens are paler, but not enough to distinguish them reliably. Song is the best guide, and the male has a very pleasant liquid song.

Willing breeders given their own space, the birds need a good insectivore diet with some seeds and fruit, and plenty of live food when breeding. Like their close relative the Silver-Eared Mesia, they will rob nests.

Active and alert, the **Pekin Robin** is the perfect introduction to keeping softbills.

Ease of care (scale 1–10)

6¼ in. (16 cm)

Planted aviary

Some heat required

May attack smaller birds

Quiet

3–5 eggs

14 days incubation

Blue-Winged Siva

(Minia cyanouroptera)

The **Blue-Winged Siva** is another charming beginner species.

Ranging through a large part of India, Burma, Thailand, southwestern China, and Malaysia, the Blue-Winged Siva is an abundant species in the wild, although not often available for sale. Olive brown above and gray-white below, it has a gray forehead and crown, some blue on wings and tails, and a tinge of blue on the back and shoulders. There is white around the eyes and also a streak of white above each eye. The sexes are alike.

Needing some heat, they do best in sheltered accommodations. Breeding is not frequent, but has been recorded a number of times. A quiet planted flight is best where they may build a neat cup nest, well hidden. Fruit and insectivore mixture should be supplemented by some live food. Pairs bond well, and the male has a pleasant song.

Similar species

Black-Capped Siva

White-Naped Yuhina

(Yuhina bakeri)

Found in the eastern Himalayas and Assam, this, like all species of Yuhina, is a tiny bird that requires experienced hands. It is greenish-gray with a darker crown, flights, and tail, and a number of yellowish buff striations on the cheeks. The underside is paler with white buff undertail coverts. The white nape is covered by the dark crown feathers, which are erected at will to produce a crest. The sexes are alike.

The **White-Naped Yuhina** is a delightful, small insectivorous bird.

Recent years have seen this species becoming more regularly available. If it is given the right conditions, once acclimatized, it will settle well into a planted aviary with heated indoor quarters and extended lighting during long winter nights. In spite of its small size, it needs space and a high-protein diet, based on as many tiny insects as you can provide – greenfly, blackfly, fruit fly larvae – a good insectivore mixture, a commercial nectar given soaked into white cake each day, and a little fruit.

Breeding may be easier in enclosed tropical aviary surroundings where you can control the supply of hatching fly pupae and other small insects, which are vital for the first days of rearing.

Similar species

Striated Yuhina
Rufous-Vented Yuhina
Formosan Yuhina
Black-Chinned Yuhina

Ease of care (scale 1–10) 8

4 in. (10 cm)

Planted aviary

Some heat required

Good mixer

Quiet

2–3 eggs

12 days incubation

Japanese Blue Flycatcher

(Cyanoptila cyanomelaena)

The **Japanese Blue Flycatcher** is very delicate and highly insectivorous.

The Blue Flycatcher comes from Manchuria, Japan, and Korea, and migrates to Burma, Thailand, Borneo, and the Philippines. The forehead, cheeks, chin, throat, and chest are black. The crown, mantle, back, and tail are bright blue, and the wings cobalt. The lower breast and underparts are white. The female is mainly olive brown above and olive gray below, whiter toward the abdomen. They take time to establish, and require an outdoor aviary with a heated shelter in winter.

A diet of a good commercial insectivore mix and live food – fly pupae, hatching flies – is required. To succeed in breeding, you must supply abundant small live food. The species is a cavity nester, and an open-fronted nest box with a natural appearance will encourage birds to breed.

Similar species

Sapphire Flycatcher
Narcissus Flycatcher
Verditer Flycatcher

Ease of care (scale 1–10) 7

6¼ in. (16 cm)

Planted aviary

Some heat required

Good mixer

Quiet

3–5 eggs

12 days incubation

Ease of care
(scale 1–10)
6

6 in.
(15 cm)

Planted
aviary

Heating
unnecessary

Keep alone
or as pair

Quiet

4 eggs

14 days
incubation

Rufous-Bellied Niltava

(Niltava sundara)

Found eastward from the Himalayas to China and Malaysia, this lovely bird has appeared in dealers' lists surprisingly often in recent years. Always considered a rare and delicate species, suitable for the experienced keeper only, once established, it is surprisingly easy to manage. Nevertheless, you must first establish it.

Iridescent cobalt blue on the crown, nape, lower cheeks, wing shoulders, and rump, it has a black forehead, chin, and neck, while the back, mantle, and tail are deep violet. The wings are blue with black flights. The breast and underparts are rufous orange. The female is brown above, with a chestnut tail, some iridescent blue spots on the sides of the neck, and a gray band across the throat.

Once established and feeding properly, this species is best kept outside in a planted flight. It does not like warm and humid conditions, and needs space and fresh air. A diet of insectivore mixture will often be taken better if housefly

The female **Rufous-Bellied Niltava** is much duller than the spectacular male.

pupae and wax moth larvae are included in the mixture. Mealworms, though easy to obtain and avidly taken, should be limited to very few a day. Like other flycatchers, these birds like to hawk flies from a perch and often take moths at dusk.

Breeding is carried out in open-fronted boxes that have been hidden low down in vegetation. To succeed in breeding, you need to provide abundant live food.

Ease of care
(scale 1–10)
7

5½ in.
(14 cm)

Planted
aviary

Some heat
required

May attack
smaller birds

Quiet

2 eggs

14 days
incubation

Scarlet-Chested Sunbird

(Nectarinia senegalensis)

The male **Scarlet-Chested Sunbird** is very aggressive, so breeding can be difficult.

Found in Senegal and Nigeria, with eight subspecies spread across a wide area of central and southern Africa, the Scarlet-Chested is abundant in many parts of its range. Sunbirds are brilliantly colored with much iridescent green and blue. This species is mainly brown with a forehead, crown, and mustachial strip of iridescent green, and a throat and breast of intense red. The female is gray-brown above, yellow-olive below, with some mottled gray at her throat.

The Scarlet-Chested is very popular in aviculture and does well in a planted aviary, but it must have heat in winter. Compatible pairs are a problem, as the males are very aggressive. However, breeding has been achieved several times by using small baskets.

A diet of a good commercial food is essential, together with small live food, fruit flies and their larvae, and hatching house flies. Use a container from which the flies escape slowly.

Malachite Sunbird

(Nectarinia famosa)

One third of this little sunbird's length is tail. It is found in Zimbabwe and South Africa, with three subspecies spread from Senegal and Ethiopia to Natal. Mainly iridescent green with darker wings and tail, it has yellow pectoral tufts. The long, fine scimitar bill is black. The male has an eclipse plumage of gray-brown, paler below; the female is gray-brown above and buff yellow below with a shorter tail.

Once acclimatized, these birds do well in an outside flight, though they need access to warmth on winter nights. Diet consists of nectar with small flies, and their larvae and pupae. They are belligerent and difficult to establish as a pair, but breeding has been achieved in single accommodations. They need birds larger than themselves if they are kept in a mixed collection.

The stunning **Malachite Sunbird** needs specialist knowledge.

Similar species

Mariqua Sunbird
Double-Collared Sunbird

Ease of care (scale 1–10) 7

9½ in. (24 cm)

Planted aviary

Some heat required

Keep alone or as pair

Quiet

2 eggs

13 days incubation

Indian Zosterop

(Zosterops palpebrosa)

One of several species in aviculture, the tiny **Indian Zostertop** is quite delightful.

The Indian Zosterop, one of some 12 subspecies, is the most often found zosterop in aviculture. A tiny olive green and yellowish bird, it has a distinctive white eye ring that has given it its alternative name of White-Eye. The forehead is yellow in some subspecies, white in others. Sexes are alike.

The Indian Zosterop is abundant in most of its range, spread through India, Thailand, China, Malaysia, Borneo, Sumatra, and Sri Lanka.

It is easily managed, and many pairs are willing breeders given a diet of fruit – pear, orange, grape halves for them to pick at – an insectivore mixture, and small live food such as fruit flies, their larvae and pupae, and any small caterpillars. With such small birds, live food is essential for breeding success, and you will need at least twice as much as you think. The species needs single accommodations when breeding, for it is very aggressive.

Similar species

African Yellow Zosterop
Chestnut-Flanked Zosterop
Black-Capped Zosterop

Ease of care (scale 1–10) 3

4½ in. (11 cm)

Planted aviary

Some heat required

Keep alone or as pair

Quiet

2–4 eggs

12 days incubation

Small Seed Eaters

The male **Siskin** is recognizable by its bright yellow coloring and black cap. This is a charming and hardy species.

Seed-eating birds are very often the first kinds tried by an aspiring aviculturalist. Being mostly quite small, often colorful, mostly charming, not noisy, usually not aggressive, and widely available, they have much to recommend them. The several hundred species and subspecies of small seed eaters originating from the Old World fall into three clearly defined groups: waxbills (Estrildinae), true finches (Carduelinae), and weavers, which are themselves divided into four closely related subgroups of the Ploceidae. The best known cage bird, the canary, is a cardueline finch, now a rarity in its native islands and classified as a CITES Appendix 1 endangered species.

Altogether there are 123 species of true finches and 132 species of waxbills, many of which are often referred to as finches, together with 149 species of buntings, sparrows, and weavers. Add to these the many hundreds of subspecies and a vast list presents itself to the taxonomist. However, most of these birds are of no relevance to aviculture, leaving me a much more manageable number of species to describe.

A male red-headed **Gouldian Finch** displaying its spectacular plumage.

Many, if not most, of the waxbills and weavers are taken from the wild in Africa and India, where they are frequently so abundant as to be serious crop pests, and are destroyed in the thousands. One, the Red-Billed Weaver, is the most numerous bird species in the world, and is sometimes controlled, horribly, with flame throwers. However, those who risk losing their crops in an area already difficult to farm must consider weavers no better than locusts.

Trade is still allowed in African and Indian species, but no longer in Old World finches, whose numbers have declined steadily. For many years, it has been illegal to take them from the wild in the British Isles, yet they still decline here. I count myself very lucky in that I see winter flocks of goldfinches numbering several hundred each year, feeding in groups on thistle and dock so intently as virtually to ignore my presence. Yet a hundred years ago, writers described these flocks in thousands. Doubtless they would decline even more if trapping were legal, and it is up to those aviculturalists who do keep them to make sure

that these species are managed properly and not wasted. I applaud the production of strains of bird that have moved away from the wild type, as with species such as greenfinches and redpolls, in which increased size and color mutations not found in the wild have created what is almost a new, domesticated species – it is far from clear what the legal definition of domesticated stock is as regards birds.

The position of Australian species is different again, for while many are still abundant, others are less so and declining. However, whatever their status, there is a total ban on the export of wildlife, captive bred or otherwise, from Australia. Once readily available, these birds are now supplied entirely by captive breeding programs, which is perhaps as it should be.

There have also been changes in management, mostly brought about by the commercial production of small live food – mealworms in various sizes, buffalo worms, wax moths, crickets, and fruit flies. Private keepers are now, as perhaps never before, learning how to cultivate these

This female **Siskin** is a paler version of the bright yellow and black male.

of unlimited gravel, but always supply cuttlefish, both grated and on the bone.

The term "seed eater" is something of a misnomer, for today it is generally recognized that while many species will exist quite happily on a hard seed diet, most, if not all, will do better with some live food, and many will breed successfully only if given a diet containing a high percentage of live food when they are rearing chicks. A large sheaf of seeding grasses placed in an aviary will give hours of pleasure to birds and bird keeper alike. Watching your charges forage for soft half-ripe seed and the myriads of insects the grass stems contain will soon dispel any doubts you may have about their diet. Apart from this it is best to feed a mixture of small millet seeds, some small-grained canary seed, such as Canadian Canary, and brown millet spray, soaked as well as dry.

Soaked seed can be a very useful addition to the diet, left until it is just beginning to germinate when it is at its highest nutritional value. However, the process must be carried out with care. Simply placing seed in water and leaving it is asking for trouble. When preparing soaked seed, I first place the seed in a container and cover it with plain water. After 12 hours I drain it, rinse it thoroughly, and then cover it again for a further 12 hours. In warm weather I often drain and rinse more than once during the second period of soaking. After 24 hours, I drain and rinse again before leaving the damp seed in a container with drain holes to allow excess water to escape. Over the following day, I may dampen the seed again as required, by which time it should have started to germinate. With the smaller birds the only soaked seed required will be brown millet spray, but for the larger birds it is usual to have a mixture of as many as six or eight different seeds, including panicum millet, white millet, black rape, teazel, niger, and hemp.

In the main, the waxbill group usually spend their summer housed in planted flights, where

essential additions to the diet of many tiny birds, and species that were once the province of professional bird gardens are now being bred in significant numbers by amateur enthusiasts.

The successful management of any bird, particularly the tiny waxbills, is very dependent on attention to detail, especially with freshly imported stock. Some of these little birds have had a long journey from the trappers to your bird room and need careful handling, including heated quarters if they have arrived during the winter months in a temperate climate. They have probably been through a quarantine period, followed by several changes of hands before they reach their final home. Often we have no way of knowing their age or, with some species, their sex. At this stage they must be handled carefully and with great consideration if they are to establish themselves.

Clean quarters, the opportunity to bathe – many are enthusiastic bathers – a high-quality diet, and plenty of live food for the little waxbills and wild seeds for the larger finches are all essential. Gravel is considered necessary by many, but other authorities believe it is less so; some even consider it dangerous. I am not an advocate they can supplement – but only supplement – their diet of seeds with insects gleaned from the plants and perhaps from a turf floor. Their live food requirement when rearing young can be staggering. Before the days of live food suppliers and the expansion of home-bred fruit fly, white worm, and mealworm colonies, it was difficult, to say the least. Many would-be breeders saw chicks deserted in the nest or thrown out by their despairing parents. I have spent many hours thrashing hedges and weeds, or shaking garden plants into an upturned umbrella in an often vain attempt to provide enough insects for a brood of demanding little birds who appear to eat three or four times their own weight in food each day.

Old World finches are less dependent on an insect diet, but certainly need a more varied diet than commercially produced hard seed, for example dandelion, dock, evening primrose, seeding grasses, fruits, and berries. Bullfinches in particular love pyracantha (firethorn) berries and will gorge themselves on them. Honeysuckle berries are also a great favorite after they have been frosted. Redpolls and siskins will spend hours feeding on alder cones and silver birch seed

tassels. I am perhaps fortunate in that I live in an area where these tree seeds are readily available, as are crops of wild teazel, dock, and wild meadow grass. Caged birds never seem to attain the color of their wild brethren, but given enough opportunities to feed on these foods, they will go some way toward it without the need for color feeding agents, which often harden, rather than enhance, feather color and texture.

With such a vast choice of small finches available, the bird keeper may be spoiled for choice. Depending on the size of your establishment, the time available to you, and the degree of experience you have, there is something for everyone in this group. I have kept many, but not all, and find pleasure in all of them, be they common or rare. A bird does not have to be colorful to be a thing of beauty. The tiny St. Helena Waxbill at first sight is a plain little bird, but on closer examination will be found to be finely detailed and prettily marked. The less flashy and plainer colored species often have such charming and confiding ways as to win you over completely, if only you take the time to look and learn.

Two **Diamond Sparrows**, displaying their attractive and easily-recognizable markings. In captivity, these birds require plenty of space.

Ease of care (scale 1–10)

4¾–5¼ in. (12–13 cm)

Planted aviary

Some heat required

Good mixer

Quiet

3–5 eggs

12–14 days incubation

Green-Winged Pytilia

(Pytilia melba)

The Green-Winged Pytilia, also known as the Melba Finch, has 10 described subspecies and occurs in Africa from Ethiopia to the Transvaal. It is a bird of the undergrowth and bushes, feeding on small insects and grasses. The bird is yellowish-gray with a red face and tail, olive upper parts, barred gray underparts, red tail, and a fine-pointed red beak, indicating a preference for an insect-based diet. Individuals are easily sexed, as the female is generally paler and lacks the red on the head. This species has the doubtful honor of being parasitized by the Paradise Whydah.

A diet based on millet and small canary seed must be supplemented by regular supplies of small live food: mini-mealworms and wax moth larvae, fruit flies, and hatchling crickets. The Green-Winged Pytilia is rather more dependent on live food than the Red-Winged. Although green food is not always taken, sprouting seed is usually welcomed.

The **Green-Winged Pytilia** is a host species for the Paradise Whydah.

Established pairs will often attempt to breed, taking up residence in woven basket nests. However, as the chicks are fed exclusively on small insects in their first week or so of life, it is essential that live food is provided if they are to succeed. Failure to do so will mean the chicks will be abandoned. Pytilias are quite delicate, especially in their ability to stand wet conditions. In a temperate climate, they should be kept in an outdoor flight only during the summer months, wintering in heated indoor quarters.

Similar species

Red-Winged Pytilia

Ease of care (scale 1–10)

4¾–5¼ in. (12–13 cm)

Planted aviary

Some heat required

Good mixer

Quiet

2–3 eggs

12 days incubation

Peter's Twinspot

(Hypargos niveoguttatus)

Also known as Peter's Firefinch, this bird is an inhabitant of southeastern Africa, with five described species spread through Zaire, Zimbabwe, Kenya, Tanzania, Mozambique, and Malawi. It needs great care when first being established, but once settled will do well. The face, throat, upper breast, upper tail coverts, and rump are red, the top of the head and nape are olive, and the lower underparts are black with white spots.

This species is not common, but when it is available, it makes an excellent addition to a collection of similar-sized birds. It is not weather resistant and needs some shelter, even in summer months, with slight heat and additional lighting during the winter if kept in temperate conditions.

A diet of small seeds and insects similar to that for the Green-Winged Pytilia will ensure good health. Breeding is possible but not frequent. An

Peter's Twinspot is delicate at first, but once established will usually do well.

open-fronted nest box or woven basket placed low down in a planted flight in good cover is more likely to encourage this species to breed than one placed high up in an exposed position. When building, the Twinspot favors feathers as a lining for its basic grass-and-rootlet globe nest.

Common Firefinch

(Lagonosticta senegala)

Also called the Red-Billed Firefinch, this charming species inhabits tropical West Africa, living mainly in the drier areas. It is often seen in towns and villages, where it is trusting enough to come inside houses. It is mainly brown, suffused with red above, the lower parts shading from red to buff with a black and red tail. The bill is red, as are the legs. The female is paler with upper parts shading toward gray.

This species is by no means as dependent on insects as many others, but does benefit from some small amounts of live food added to its basic diet of small millets and canary seed. Seeding grasses and green food are a welcome addition, as are sprouting millet sprays.

The bird is abundant in the wild state and a long-established favorite in aviculture. Its confiding nature means it is likely to be a free breeder given the right conditions; it has often

The **Firefinch** can be kept at liberty in suitable areas.

been given its liberty in suitable areas where cats, sparrowhawks, and sharp-shinned hawks are not present. It is frequently found nesting in thatched roofs in its native Africa and will respond well to a nest basket placed in a rough thatch of grasses or reeds. Yet, in spite of its ease of management, it is by no means a simple species to establish, as it tends to suffer from stress when first imported.

Ease of care (scale 1–10) 2

4 in. (10 cm)

Planted aviary

Some heat required

Good mixer

Quiet

2–4 eggs

12 days incubation

Blue-Capped Cordon Bleu

(Uraeginthus cyanocephala)

The **Blue-Capped Cordon Bleu** is a lovely addition to any collection of small seed eaters.

Also known as the Blue-Headed Waxbill, the male is a striking sky blue over the whole of the head and body, only the wings and back abdomen and undertail coverts being shades of fawn and beige. Females and immature males are paler. This makes establishment of pairs initially difficult as many apparent hens turn out to be young males. Much more restricted than either the Red-Cheeked or Common Cordon Bleu, the Blue-Capped is found from Ethiopia to Tanzania.

It should be carefully acclimatized, and will become quite hardy. If the law allows, it makes an excellent liberty bird that rarely strays far. Aside from the usual mixture of millets and seeding grasses, the bird is highly insectivorous when rearing young. It will take soft food, especially if small live food such as ant eggs are folded in.

Similar species

Common Cordon Bleu
Red-Cheeked Cordon Bleu

Ease of care (scale 1–10) 2

5 in. (13 cm)

Planted aviary

Some heat required

Good mixer

Quiet

4–6 eggs

10–12 days incubation

Ease of care
(scale 1–10)
5

4¾–5½ in.
(12–14 cm)

Planted
aviary

Some heat
required

Keep alone
or as pair

Quiet

3–4 eggs

12–13 days
incubation

Violet-Eared Waxbill

(Uraeginthus grantina)

The **Violet-Eared Waxbill** is beautiful but pugnacious, and so requires its own space.

Also known as the Common Grenadier Waxbill, this bird's chestnut back and dark brown wings set off the cobalt blue head and violet sides; blue tail coverts over a black tail make this a striking little bird. The female is similar but paler. The range of the four described species is Mozambique, Natal, Cape Province, and Angola, where it is reasonably plentiful.

At one time much in demand, it has declined as an avicultural species, mainly because of its delicate nature, being always sensitive to low temperatures and damp conditions.

Showing little interest in green food, this species is strongly insectivorous, although it will do well on small millets and seeding grasses.

If you wish to try breeding, abundant small live food is essential. Potential breeding pairs must be housed separately from others of similar species, as the Grenadier become very pugnacious and territorial. Single specimens may be housed in mixed collections, when they frequently become very tame and engaging characters.

Ease of care
(scale 1–10)
2

4½–4¾ in.
(11–12 cm)

Planted
aviary

Some heat
required

Good
mixer

Quiet

3–4 eggs

11–12 days
incubation

Lavender Finch

(Estrilda caerulescens)

A well-established and very popular species in aviculture, this bird is of an overall blue-gray except for rump, tail, and legs, which are black, and the typical red waxbill beak. The sexes are alike. Ranging from Senegal to the Central African Republic, the Lavender Finch has no described subspecies.

A diet of millet spray, seeding grasses, and live food is required, and the bird will also take some green food.

Lavender Finches are relatively free breeders, provided you can establish a true pair. Given the right long-stemmed grasses, they will build their own funnel nest, but they will also accept a woven basket nest or an open-fronted box, tucked into cover. When rearing chicks, they must have access to abundant live food, fruit flies, tiny housefly larvae, chopped mealworms, and greenfly. Once established, they will do well in an outdoor flight

The **Lavender Finch's** soft coloring reflects its quiet, confiding nature.

with a shelter, but must be kept indoors during winter months with slight heat and additional light. Failing an indoor flight, a flight cage and lots to do will keep this active bird in good order.

Orange-Cheeked Waxbill

(Estrilda melpoda)

This bird has brown wings and a fawn upper body, with gray/fawn head, nape, and breast, and the orange cheeks that give the species its name. The underparts are gray and the tail black. It is difficult to sex as the birds are quite variable, although the females often have smaller areas of orange on the cheeks and are somewhat duller. The two described species are found in Gambia, Zaire, Chad, Cameroon, and North Angola. It is very abundant and a serious crop pest over much of its range.

It thrives on millet spray, including sprouted seed and weed seeds, together with some green

The **Orange-Cheeked Waxbill** is difficult to sex, some individuals more so than others.

food. In season I give large bunches of seeding grasses, which give the birds the opportunity to show off their acrobatic quality. Small insects are acceptable, but this little bird is less reliant than many others on live food, except when breeding. Given enough live food, a pair will produce several broods of chicks; but once the young are independent, they should be removed, or they will all sit in the nest with the brooding parent, reducing the chance of a second brood to nil.

It is established relatively easily and is a good mixer; small groups give this gregarious species an opportunity to show its charms, though you must watch out for bullies. Relatively hardy, it will spend the summer months happily outside, but it requires shelter and extra light during the dark winter months.

Similar species

Red-Eared Waxbill
Swee Waxbill

Ease of care (scale 1–10) 1

4–4½ in. (10–11 cm)

Planted aviary

Some heat required

Good mixer

Quiet

5–6 eggs

11–12 days incubation

St. Helena Waxbill

(Estrilda astrild)

Also known as the Common Waxbill, there are 17 described subspecies of this bird, covering a very large area from Sudan to Cape Province. The bird is fawn brown on the upper surface lined with fine darker brown stripes, and has a whitish chin and a grayish breast colored pink toward the center, darkening toward the underparts. The tail and undercoverts are black. There is a red eye

streak. The sexes are much alike, but the female is paler and usually has less red on the belly.

This waxbill does well on a seed and insect diet, like others in the family. It is much easier to establish than most, usually arriving in feather-perfect condition. Common it may be, worthwhile it most certainly is. The St. Helena is very active and expressive, and there are few species that have such a neat appearance.

It can be a very free breeder, using a globe nest placed low down in natural cover or bundles of dried grass. In the wild, it is regularly parasitized by the Pin-Tailed Whydah (*Vidua macroura*), as is the Red-Eared Waxbill. The chicks of the Pin-Tailed mimic those of the waxbill in their throat markings, and it is likely that both chicks are reared together. I have never had personal experience of this.

The **St. Helena** is a jaunty little bird, delicately marked and almost always in perfect feather.

Ease of care (scale 1–10) 1

3½–4½ in. (9–11 cm)

Planted aviary

Some heat required

Good mixer

Quiet

4–6 eggs

11–13 days incubation

Ease of care (scale 1–10)

 3½– 4¾ in. (9–12 cm)

 Planted aviary

 Some heat required

 Good mixer

 Quiet

 4–6 eggs

 11–13 days incubation

Red Avadavat

(Amandava amandava)

Unlike the previous waxbills, this species comes from India, not Africa. There are two distinct races, the larger often known as the Bombay Avadavat, and the smaller and more brightly colored called the Tiger Finch or, very appropriately, Strawberry Finch. Hens are a pale gray brown above and yellowish gray below, spotted here and there. The males have two plumages, a breeding and an eclipse plumage, which are strikingly different. In eclipse they resemble the females, but in breeding order they are a bright dark red with white spots, living up to the name of Strawberry Finch. If fed on a diet of seed only, the male will turn almost black when changing to breeding plumage. Given a planted natural flight and access to an insect diet, it will revert to the true red color the following season.

This is the only waxbill with a true song, and the males produce a very sweet, if somewhat monotonous song, like the tinkling of a tiny silver bell. Mixing well with other species of waxbill, the Red Avadavat is a charming and deservedly popular little bird. It can be pugnacious toward others with red in their plumage and is particularly aggressive when nesting. I have bred this species in a cage, but it can be hard work providing enough insects.

The diet is as for other waxbills: millets, seeding grasses with germinated millet spray, and a plentiful supply of small live food when rearing chicks.

The Red Avadavat is easy to establish, quite hardy, and is often claimed to be hardy enough to winter outside in a cool climate. However, it is best if the bird is given warm dry quarters to overwinter rather than subject it to the rigors of long, dark, freezing nights.

Similar species

Green Avadavat

This male **Red Avadavat** is coming into nuptial plumage.

Golden-Breasted Waxbill

(Amandava subflava)

There are two described species of this tiny waxbill, the larger of the two being referred to as the Orange-Breasted. It is usually the smaller that is imported. It is abundant in many parts of a large range that extends from the Sudan to South Africa. The head and upper surfaces are dark gray-green while the underparts are barred yellow. There is a red eye stripe, and the bill is also red. The female is duller and paler.

This is the smallest of the waxbills, but its tiny size is deceptive, for it is very robust. It is an excellent subject and often quite free breeding, depending, like most of its relatives, on a good supply of small insects and germinated seeds while rearing young.

It will do well in a planted flight, but care should be taken to see that this little bird is not

The male **Golden-Breasted Waxbill** is much brighter than the female.

bullied. It usually likes a globe nest placed close to the ground in thick vegetation or bundles of grasses. It will breed in a flight cage, but does need some form of cover over the nest area, such as bundles of hay or straw giving the appearance of natural vegetation. Slight heat and inside accommodations are required during the winter.

 Ease of care (scale 1–10)
 3½ in. (9 cm)
 Planted aviary
 Some heat required
 Good mixer
 Quiet
 4–5 eggs
 11–12 days incubation

Diamond Sparrow

(Emblema guttata)

This handsome bird inhabits the west central to southeastern part of Australia. Also known as the Diamond Firetail, it has a silvery gray head and nape with a brown back and wings, a red rump, and a black tail. The sides of the head are grayish with the underparts white. The breast is marked with a black band, and the sides and flanks are also black with large white spots. A red bill and feet set off this ensemble. The female is similar but smaller. There is only one described species.

In captivity, it requires a large flight cage or an aviary enclosure if it is to succeed as a breeding bird, for it is active and prone to feather plucking if confined. It is otherwise easily managed and breeds well, which is fortunate with no wild birds available to supplement our captive stocks. A large, messy sparrowlike nest often overspills any

The popular **Diamond Sparrow** is not actually a sparrow at all.

nest box, and it will build from scratch if given a suitable site. This bird has always been popular, but is sadly in decline in its native habitat.

A diet of canary seed, mixed millets, and spray millet, some green food, and seeding grasses are favored. If breeding, it needs extra millet spray and germinated seeds, plus some live food in the form of buffalo worms and mini-mealworms. They can be aggressive when housed in mixed groups and so should be isolated when breeding.

Similar species

Painted Finch

 Ease of care (scale 1–10)
 4¾–5 in. (12–13 cm)
 Planted aviary
 Some heat required
 Keep alone or as pair
 Quiet
 4–6 eggs
 11–13 days incubation

 Ease of care
(scale 1–10)

 4½–4¾ in.
(11–12 cm)

 Planted
aviary

 Some heat
required

 Good
mixer

 Quiet

 3–5 eggs

 12–13 days
incubation

Star Finch

(Neochima ruficauda)

This popular and widely kept grass finch occurs naturally in most of the northern areas of Australia, where its two described species vary greatly in numbers. Agriculture appears to improve its chances. The red face and olive breast and sides are covered with tiny white spots, giving this bird its name. The brilliant red of the face and head is not so extensive in the female, and young birds are olive green. Some authors state that young males often take several years to color up, but others, including myself, have not found this to be the case.

Given the right conditions and plenty of live food, greenfly being a favorite and readily taken, they are model parents and will breed very well. They have been known to hybridize with their close relative the Crimson Finch (*Neochima*

The **Star Finch** is slightly less hardy than many small finches, but is still popular.

phaeton), which should be discouraged. Hybrids reduce the purity of our captive stocks.

General management is as for the Diamond Sparrow, although the Star Finch is slightly less hardy than the Diamond.

 Ease of care
(scale 1–10)

 5½–6¾ in.
(14–17 cm)

 Planted
aviary

 Heating
unnecessary

 May attack
smaller birds

 Quiet

 5–6 eggs

 11–13 days
incubation

Long-Tailed Grass Finch

(Poephila acuticauda)

With the exception of the Zebra Finch, the Long-Tailed is probably the most numerous of all the Australian finches. It may be quickly distinguished from its close relative, the Masked Grass Finch, by the large black bib extending down to the breast and the longer tail with its extended central feathers. There are two races:

The handsome, bold **Long-Tailed Grass Finch** may be cage bred.

those from the east have yellow beaks, while the less common western race have red beaks. It is the western subspecies that is usually called Heck's Grass Finch. The head is pale silvery gray with the rest of the upper surface a warm fawn brown with a rosy tinge. The white rump has a black band across the top, extending underneath.

Long-Tailed Grass Finches should be kept on a diet of canary and mixed millet, millet spray, and green food. Live food is essential for breeding birds. Most birds will breed in an indoor flight or box cage; they are quite aggressive and need to be housed separately when breeding. They are hardy and can be wintered outside if given good shelter at night, but they are best housed inside in temperate climates. Damp weather does not suit them, and they are prone to pneumonia. Established pairs can be extremely prolific, while others seem to get everything wrong and can be infuriating.

Similar species

**Parson Finch
Masked Grass Finch
Bichino Finch**

Ease of care
(scale 1–10)

4½– 4¾ in.
(11–12 cm)

Planted
aviary

Heating
unnecessary

Good
mixer

Quiet

3–6 eggs

12–13 days
incubation

Zebra Finch

(Poephila guttata)

The **Zebra Finch** is virtually domesticated now with dozens of mutations to choose from.

Also known as the Chestnut-Eared Finch, a description of this little Australian bird is almost superfluous, even if one ignores the many color mutations that have been produced, and those that may still yet appear. In the normal type, the top of the head, nape, and back are gray, and there are fawn-gray wings, chestnut cheek patches, and a vertical black stripe from eye to bib. The chin, throat, and sides of the neck are barred black and white, a band of black across the breast with white below. The chestnut flanks are heavily spotted white, and the tail is barred in black and white. The bill and legs are bright red. The female lacks the chestnut cheek patches, flanks, and barred breast. We are now treated to an amazing variety of mutation colors, which include fawns, whites, black-breasted and chestnut-flanked whites, pieds, and many others.

The Zebra Finch has its own specialist society and is bred as a show bird, with a standard of excellence difficult for the amateur to achieve. Indeed, it has been said that the Zebra is one of the most difficult birds to breed to show standard. Show or pet, the species is readily, not to say

commonly, available. This should not deter a potential keeper, for it is a worthwhile and rewarding species. I well remember my first Zebra Finches, which I bought from a distant dealer: their arrival by rail, their subsequent escape from the traveling box into my birdroom (fortunately secure), and the almost instant playing of the toy trumpet that is the male bird's song, seeming like a challenge to "catch me if you can." It is probably the perfect beginner's species.

Zebra Finches will breed throughout the year if allowed, although their habit of making egg sandwiches by building nest after nest on top of each fresh clutch can be infuriating. They are best bred in cages as single-species pairs if controlled results are required, for they frequently interfere with other birds' nesting attempts if placed in a mixed collection. If aviary breeding is desired, my favorite method is to suspend sheaves of long grasses from perches and aviary sides, giving natural breeding sites as an alternative to wicker nest baskets. A diet of mixed millet and canary seed, plus millet spray and some green food will do very well.

 Ease of care (scale 1–10) **4**

 4½–5 in. (11–13 cm)

 Planted aviary

 Some heat required

 Keep alone or as pair

 Quiet

 3–6 eggs

 12–14 days incubation

Blue-Faced Parrot Finch

(Erythrura trichroa)

The forehead, face, and cheeks are blue; the crown, back, and wings are grass green, as are the underparts; it has a red rump, and brown and red tail; the beak is black. This species has 11 described races from New Guinea and the Celebes to Northern Australia, where it is now virtually absent. Habitat loss is generally the cause of its decline, as with so many other birds.

The Blue-Faced Parrot Finch does best on a diet of mixed millet seeds with spray millet and seeding grasses. Some live food is taken and is required in abundance when breeding.

It is generally a nervous species, but it can be encouraged to breed freely if given space and careful management. It needs shelter and a degree of seclusion when breeding, and warm quarters with extended daylight during winter months.

The **Blue-Faced Parrot Finch** is nervous, but can be encouraged to be free breeding.

Similar species

Red-Headed Parrot Finch
Pin-Tailed Parrot Finch

 Ease of care (scale 1–10) **4**

 4¾–5 in. (12–13 cm)

 Planted aviary

 Some heat required

 Good mixer

 Quiet

 3–8 eggs

 12–13 days incubation

Gouldian Finch

(Chloebia gouldiae)

The Gouldian is unusual in that it has three distinct forms in the wild: red, black, and yellow-headed. The demarcation of colors in the one bird is quite breathtaking. It breeds well in cage or aviary, and a number of mutations are well established, none of which, in my view, come near to the dazzling beauty of the original color forms. In some parts of its Australian homeland, it is an endangered species.

The **Gouldian Finch** has three natural color forms and several avicultural mutations.

The basic seed diet is a mixture of small canary seed and millet, although it is important to provide soaked seed, along with egg food and green food, and some live food throughout the rearing season. Cuttlefish should be provided rather than gravel; the species seems to need a lot of calcium. Care must be taken when youngsters are being weaned, as they are very prone to "going light."

Although Gouldians may be kept in an outside flight during summer months in temperate climates, they must be given heated quarters in winter with extended light, for they will frequently breed during winter months. The young birds are surprisingly drab at first, being green all over, and take several months to color up, although the bright breast feathers appear soon after fledging.

Since they live in small colonies in the wild, they can be kept as single-species groups, or used to mix into an aviary group of similar-sized birds. In some parts of the world, they have been cage bred in vast numbers, producing many new mutations; often, though, these birds have proved to be very weak.

Cherry Finch

(Aidemosyne modesta)

The **Cherry Finch** is a bird of quiet charm and shy manner.

This Australian finch of quiet charm is found in western Queensland and New South Wales. It is also known as the Plum-Headed Finch. I must own up to a special feeling for this little bird of subdued colors and shy manners. The forehead is dark plum red, the upper body brown with white spots on wings and tail. The underparts are brown and white. There is a very pretty fawn mutation even more muted in color. The female is similar, but the area of plum color on the head is smaller.

A diet of small canary seeds and mixed millets, with spray millet, seeding grasses, and some green food is required. When rearing young, mini-mealworms, buffalo worms, egg food, and germinated seed are required.

Not widely kept and certainly less robust than it looks, this small finch is quite delicate and can be difficult to establish. It will breed in a large flight cage, but needs cover and seclusion as the parent birds are often very nervous when breeding and will desert chicks if they are stressed. Like most other related birds, it does not like cold, damp conditions during winter months.

Ease of care (scale 1–10) 2

4½–4¾ in. (11–12 cm)

Planted aviary

Some heat required

Good mixer

Quiet

3–6 eggs

12–13 days incubation

African Silverbill

(Lonchura cantans)

This Silverbill ranges over large areas of the drier parts of Africa, where it is generally abundant. It is pale brown above and pale buff below, the wings are dark brown, the tail black, and the bill blue-gray. The sexes are identical, and it is best to judge by the song. It prefers canary and mixed millets with additional spray millet, seeding grasses, and some green food. Live food is taken when young are being reared, but often they will do very well without.

This species is inexpensive and breeds freely, either in a cage or a planted aviary. If established in a cage, it does need some seclusion and cover to succeed. The male bird is happier if given space to stand guard over his mate by sitting on top of the nest. It is not uncommon for the Silverbill to try to take over the nest of another species, evicting the owner. Every successful species tends to be strong-willed, and this bird is no exception.

The **African Silverbill** is one of the recommended beginner species.

Once established, it can be quite hardy, but requires dry, frost-free quarters in winter.

It is said of the closely related Indian Silverbill that it sets up home in the nests of larger birds, such as eagles. This would be no surprise, as birds of prey tend to ignore tiny birds such as these.

Similar species

Indian Silverbill

Ease of care (scale 1–10) 1

4½–4¾ in. (11–12 cm)

Planted aviary

Some heat required

May attack smaller birds

Quiet

3–8 eggs

10–11 days incubation

The **Bronze Mannikin** is very popular in aviculture, and is readily available.

Ease of care (scale 1–10) — 1

3½–4 in. (9–10 cm)

Planted aviary

Some heat required

Good mixer

Quiet

4–8 eggs

11–12 days incubation

Bronze Mannikin

(Lonchura culcullata)

Three races of this mannikin inhabit a large part of east and west Africa, some islands, and south into Angola and South Africa. The head, upper wing, and sides are black with iridescent green, while the throat and upper breast are black, suffused with bronze and green. The nape, back, and main wing area are brown tinged with gray, while the underparts are white. Flanks and tail coverts are barred with black. The sexes are alike, but can be distinguished by display and song.

Their preferred diet is canary seed and mixed millet, with spray millet, germinated seed, green food, and some live food when breeding.

A very popular avicultural species, the Bronze is a fairly good mixer, although a little bossy. A small colony is often best as they are happy to roost together, sometimes in a heap in a nest box. They will breed well if left to work out their own domestic arrangements. They are hardy once settled in, although frost-free quarters are a must.

Similar species

Tri-Colored Mannikin
Black-Headed Mannikin
White-Headed Mannikin
Spice Bird
Pictorella Finch

Ease of care (scale 1–10) — 1

5 in. (13 cm)

Cage

Heating unnecessary

Good mixer

Quiet

3–8 eggs

12–14 days incubation

Bengalese Mannikin

(Domestic)

No one is really certain as to the origins of this little mannikin, but it is generally regarded as a domesticated form of the White-Backed Mannikin, *Lonchura striata*. Also known as the Society Finch, there are three basic color forms and a number of variations on the theme of chocolate, fawn, and white, plus a crested form. As with the Zebra Finch, there is a society dedicated solely to breeding this species. A mix of canary seed and millets with spray millet, seeding grasses, and green food keeps birds in good health.

Bengalese are very free breeders and are often used to foster eggs and chicks of other seed-eating species of similar size. They do best in cages and indoor flights rather than outdoor aviaries. Bengalese are often so eager to breed and rear chicks they will take over other birds' nests, to the real owners' consternation.

Not found in the wild, the **Bengalese Mannikin** is a truly domesticated species.

Java Sparrow

(Padda oryzivora)

Also known as a Paddy Bird, in the wild type, the whole of the head, nape, and chin are black with bold white cheeks. The back, wings, and breast are blue-gray, and the tail and primary feathers are black. The bill is pink. There are four separate color forms – white, fawn, and pied (gray/white and fawn/white). The species is found from Java to the coast of East Africa, with a number of introduced birds expanding the range.

In addition to the usual mix of canary seed and millet, this bird enjoys unhusked rice and green food. The species is an old favorite with a very long history in aviculture. It needs single accommodations when breeding and will use a large open nest box in which to build its straggly nest. It is unusual to find healthy birds in anything other than perfect feather. They are not safe to mix with smaller birds, but can be safely placed with birds of equal size or larger.

The **Java Sparrow** is an old favorite in aviculture. This is the normal form.

 Ease of care (scale 1–10) 1

 5–6 in. (13–15 cm)

 Cage

 Heating unnecessary

 May attack smaller birds

 Quiet

 3–6 eggs

 11–12 days incubation

Cut-Throat Finch

(Amadina fasciata)

There are four described subspecies of this well-known and abundant avicultural bird, ranging across Africa from Ethiopia to the Transvaal, the most usual cage bird being from Senegal and Uganda. The red band across the throat of the male bird gives it its name and is an immediate point of identification. It is also known as a Ribbon Finch. The general color otherwise is gray-brown, the upper surface covered with fine barring. The underparts are yellowish fawn, with darker margins giving a scale effect. The female is similar except for not having a red throat band.

The preferred diet is canary and mixed millet seeds, plus millet spray, with green food. Added egg food, germinated seed, and some insects are desirable for breeding birds, although they will succeed without.

Cut-Throats breed freely once established. They are, however, pugnacious and should not be housed with small waxbills. Although I have never

A band of red under the chin marks out the male **Cut-Throat Finch**.

 Ease of care (scale 1–10) 1

 4¾–5 in. (12–13 cm)

 Cage

 Some heat required

 May attack smaller birds

 Quiet

 4–6 eggs

 11–12 days incubation

heard of them killing other birds, I have also never given them the chance, for they can be persistent bullies. They can be safely housed with budgerigars in an aviary but, if cage breeding is your aim, they should be alone. Hens confined in cages can be subject to egg binding, so they need to be fit and lean before beginning the season. They are gregarious outside the breeding season.

Ease of care
(scale 1–10)
4

6 in.
(15 cm)

Planted
aviary

Heating
unnecessary

Keep alone
or as pair

Quiet

3–5 eggs

13–14 days
incubation

Chaffinch

(Fringilla coelebs)

This was the first of the Old World finches to be described. In Britain, keepers should be aware that this species, along with all other native finches, is protected by the Wildlife and Countryside Act 1981 (Schedule 3 part 1), and only close-ringed, aviary-bred birds may be offered for sale.

The bird is found throughout Europe, but is widespread throughout most of the Old World, with 14 races described. The head and nape are steel blue; the face, throat, mantle, and underparts are browny pink, shading to grayish white on the abdomen. The wings are brown with a white wing bar, and the tail is dark gray with the two outer feathers white. The female is similar but paler, with a much narrower white wing bar and lacking the blue head. As the males age, their color improves yearly until they reach about seven years, after which it begins to fade.

The male Chaffinch was once kept as a song bird, and still is in Belgium, where the birds are judged by the number of full song patterns repeated in a given period. Shortened phrases are discounted; only the complete, albeit short, bursts of song are considered valid.

The diet is of mixed seeds based on a good canary mixture with added wild seeds and green food. Wild seeds collected from safe areas – those free from pesticide sprays and other fouling – are beneficial, as is small live food.

This is a nervous species, best in a well planted aviary with plenty of cover. It is not as free breeding as some; potential breeding birds should be kept as a single pair in a small flight, for they are generally pugnacious. Vast amounts of live food, as well as extra green food and germinated seeds, are required when breeding, for the species is chiefly insectivorous when rearing young.

The male **Chaffinch** at nest, which includes many cobwebs and lichens in its construction.

Greenfinch

(Carduelis chloris)

A splendid male **Greenfinch** with bright yellow wing bands.

This very common European species is abundant in many parts of its range, which extends into Siberia. It is olive green above with yellowish green underparts. The wings have a broad yellow bar, and the outer tail feathers are also yellow. The female is grayer, and the yellow is much reduced. Several color mutations are now well established, including cinnamon, lutino, and isabel (brownish-gray).

A diet of mixed canary and wild seeds with green food ad lib, is preferred.

Greenfinches are very free breeding; they were my first breeding finches, as with many a novice before and since. They will breed in a cage or a flight, but need artificial cover with wicker or wire nest supports well tucked away. They are usually good mixers, continuing with their own business and ignoring all other birds, except at feeding stations where they tend to be a trifle bossy. They will often rear chicks on hard seed and green food alone, but do better with some egg food, germinated seeds, and a little live food, blackfly and greenfly being taken if offered.

The chicks can often be very difficult to wean, suffering from "going light" syndrome, which is still not fully understood. Sulfur drugs are still the best method of controlling the problem, together with isolation in clinically clean cages.

Ease of care (scale 1–10)

5½–6¼ in. (14–16 cm)

Planted aviary

Heating unnecessary

Good mixer

Quiet

4–6 eggs

12–14 days incubation

Siskin

(Carduelis spinus)

The bright colors and black cap of the male **Siskin** makes identification simple.

Small and active, this little finch is full of charm and very confiding. It is not much of a songster, but what it lacks in music is made up for in many other ways. The crown of the head and chin are black, the upper surfaces streaked black over olive green. Wings and tail are black with two distinct yellow wing bars. The underparts are yellow-green, fading toward the abdomen. The female is paler and lacks the black cap.

Diet should be mixed seeds, taking care not to overdo fatty and oily seeds, for these birds quickly become overweight if allowed to gorge on hemp seed, for example. Include green food ad lib and wild seeds where possible. I frequently collect the seed heads of silver birch and alder trees especially for my Siskins who, like their wild brethren, spend many hours swinging on the branches like titmice.

An easily managed species, they mix well, but a better breeding rate will be achieved if they are treated as a single group. Coming from northern Europe, they are completely hardy.

Ease of care (scale 1–10)

4¾ in. (12 cm)

Planted aviary

Heating unnecessary

Good mixer

Quiet

3–5 eggs

12 days incubation

Ease of care
(scale 1–10)
2

5½ in.
(14 cm)

Planted
aviary

Heating
unnecessary

Good
mixer

Quiet

4–6 eggs

10–12 days
incubation

Linnet

(Acanthis flammea)

The male is gray-brown above with darker striations, chestnut back and wings, and a pinkish breast when in breeding condition. In some specimens the forehead will also color up pink. The female is similar, but lacks the pink areas. The species is found throughout Europe, Asia, and North Africa.

This a very popular species, though nervous. It has long been kept for its song, and until the 19th century many households had a linnet in a cage. More freely breeding than the Chaffinch, it does well in a flight with plenty of cover, but not so well in a cage, where it often develops the disconcerting habit of turning over backward on a show-cage perch. The remedy for this used to be to put in a wire perch threaded through the stem of a clay pipe, which turned around if the bird tried to spin over and soon taught it to sit up properly. Diet should be mixed seeds, including rape seed, niger, and wild seeds. Green food is essential.

To show its pink breast in captivity, the **Linnet** needs color feeding.

Ease of care
(scale 1–10)
3

7½ in.
(19 cm)

Planted
aviary

Heating
unnecessary

Keep alone
or as pair

Quiet

3–5 eggs

14–16 days
incubation

Hawfinch

(Coccothraustes coccothraustes)

A powerful bill capable of cracking cherry stones identifies the **Hawfinch**.

Found throughout Europe and into Asia, the Hawfinch is the largest of the Old World finches, and with its huge beak is a bird which, once seen, is never forgotten. The striking bill varies in color according to the time of year. Bright chestnut head and neck, dark brown back, blue-black flight feathers, and a well defined wing bar, a black bib, and pale pinkish-brown breast and abdomen make this a very striking bird. The hen is paler, and the black bib is not as large.

A diet high in sunflower seed is preferred with a basic canary mixture, and various fruits and berries, including hawthorn and pyracantha. Soft food, mealworms, greenfood, sprouting seed, and ant eggs are all taken when rearing young. The chicks leave the nest at 12 or 13 days, so they need a very high protein diet.

This powerful finch should be housed in a deep secluded aviary with plenty of cover, if for no other reason than that the males are so dominant. The female needs cover to escape the forceful attention of her mate.

Bullfinch

(Pyrrhula pyrrhula)

The face, crown, and bib are black, as are the tail and flight feathers. The nape and back are soft gray, and the breast and flanks are rose pink. The rump is white and the bill black. The female is duller and much browner, and less well marked than the male. There are several races of this charming species spread through Europe and Asia as far as Korea. The male has the most delightful habit of swinging his tail from side to side as he sings a very soft song, which may include some phrases learned from other species. A German Kaiser had a bird that repeated the notes of his famous klaxon car horn, and Bullfinches were once trained to sing with a little flute. I had an exhibition bird that learned an indistinct version of "Hello" from a pet budgie.

Diet should be a good mix of seeds based on canary mixture with added berries in season – especially when molting, where blackberries and pyracantha berries will do much to aid the retention of the wonderful rose-pink breast. Wild seeds and green food are a must, and soft fruit may be offered.

Wild Bullfinches are notorious for the damage they do to the buds of fruit trees, but not being a fruit grower I can forgive this delightful and confiding finch, for which I have a very soft spot. They breed freely in a planted flight or a flight cage with lots of artificial cover. They are difficult in that they often do not accept the close ringing of their chicks, throwing baby out with the bathwater in an attempt to remove the rings, which they perceive as foreign bodies in the nest. Live food is important for at least part of the rearing period, and ant eggs and greenfly are much appreciated. Bullfinches do best as single species, for the male is dominant and aggressive. I have known many that have killed canaries.

The lovely but pugnacious **Bullfinch** may require color feeding to retain its pink breast.

Ease of care (scale 1–10)   3

4½–6 in. (14–15 cm)

Planted aviary

Heating unnecessary

Keep alone or as pair

Quiet

4–6 eggs

14 days incubation

Ease of care
(scale 1–10)

6¼ in.
(16 cm)

Planted
aviary

Heating
unnecessary

May attack
smaller birds

Quiet

3–6 eggs

12–14 days
incubation

Pin-Tailed Whydah

(Vidua macroura)

Spreading from Ethiopia to Senegal and into Cape Province, this species is a typical whydah with a striking and dramatic variation in eclipse to breeding plumage. Outside the breeding season the sexes are alike – small, brown-striated and plain brown birds – although the male is more boldly marked and slightly larger. From July the males assume their breeding plumage, a new suit of shining black and white, including an elongated tail. Whydahs were collectively known as "widow birds," because the long tail resembles black trailing ribbons. The species is common in all parts of tropical Africa other than desert or forest, and its tail feathers were used for head-dresses. The older the bird, frequently the longer the tail feathers and the longer the period "in color." The return to eclipse plumage, generally in December or January, appears to be completed without a molt. In spite of its tropical origin the Pin-Tailed is very hardy once acclimatized.

These whydahs are best kept in groups of several females to one male, for the male is polygamous. The species does not pair and nest; rather, it is parasitic, laying in the nests of small estrildian finches if conditions are right. As the male is extremely pugnacious, this species should only be included with birds of equal or larger size, or the smaller waxbills if the aviary size allows plenty of space for the small finches to stay out of his way. Failure to allow for this will result in certain death for any bird who makes the error of being in the wrong place at the wrong time. The bird's habit of scratching around on the aviary floor like a tiny chicken attracts other occupants hoping for a free meal, and camp followers are only tolerated for just so long. Having said this, a number of captive breedings have been recorded.

The courtship display alone is worthy of additional space for this and any other whydah species, for it is only when given adequate room that the full beauty of the display can be seen. The male engages in aerobatics, twisting and turning to show off his streamer tail and hovering over a hen before returning to his perch, to repeat the performance again and again.

A diet of canary and mixed millet seeds is usual, with germinated seeds a welcome addition. Any chicks produced in the hosts' nests are fed on small insects by their foster parents.

This **Pin-Tailed Whydah** has a very long tail in nuptial plumage.

Ease of care (scale 1–10)

16 in. (40 cm)

Planted aviary

Heating unnecessary

May attack smaller birds

Quiet

3–6 eggs

12–14 days incubation

Paradise Whydah

(Vidua paradisaea)

A male **Paradise Whydah** with his splendid tail in full breeding plumage.

Next to the Pin-Tailed, this whydah is the most commonly imported from its extensive habitat in northern, central, and southern Africa. Similar to the Pin-Tailed in eclipse plumage, the Paradise Whydah changes to black above with a band of golden buff across the nape and a chestnut breast fading to pale buff on the abdomen. The striking black tail is composed of two elements. Two feathers are wide and short, and raised like a fan, while two greatly elongated and flowing feathers complete the train. Out of "color," the sexes are similar: a black crown with a central brown streak, yellow-brown streaked upper parts, and grayish white below. Frequently available, it is widely kept and quite hardy.

Like the Pin-Tailed, the Paradise Whydah is parasitic, the host being the Melba Finch. It is rather less pugnacious, but still needs space and careful watching. Some breeding success has been recorded, the main difficulty being to maintain enough host pairs for the breeding times to coincide. It is not a species that does well in cages; it needs space, especially when carrying its full tail. Management is as for the Pin-Tailed Whydah.

Similar species

Broad-Tailed Whydah
Queen Whydah

Ease of care
(scale 1–10)

4¾ in.
(12 cm)

Planted
aviary

Some heat
required

Good
mixer

Quiet

3–6 eggs

12–14 days
incubation

Combassou

(Vidua chalybeata)

The steel-colored **Combassou** lacks the long tail of other whydahs.

It comes as a surprise to many to learn that this small bird is a member of the family of whydahs or widow birds, lacking as it does the elongated tail feathers, so much a feature of most of its relatives. Six subspecies are spread across Africa from Ethiopia to Zimbabwe and Mozambique. In breeding plumage the male is a glossy black with a metallic navy blue gloss, except for the primary feathers, which are plain black, the whole offset by a pale pink beak. Outside the breeding season, the male and female are alike, striated brown above with buff underparts. It is also known as a Steel Finch or Indigo Bird.

Diet consists of equal parts of canary seed, white and panicum millet, together with millet sprays, green food, and some live food.

Less often available than they once were, as is the case with most whydahs, they are still popular with aviculturalists. One cause of their decline is perhaps that they are rarely bred in captivity, for they are mainly parasitic on the Red-Billed Firefinch, although there are examples of pairs rearing their own offspring. If you are planning to breed this species, you should consider including firefinches in the collection. In other respects, this species is a good mixer and easily managed.

Ease of care
(scale 1–10)

12 in.
(30 cm)

Planted
aviary

Some heat
required

May attack
smaller birds

Quiet

3–6 eggs

12–14 days
incubation

Fischer's Whydah

(Vidua fischeri)

This whydah is found in Ethiopia, Somalia, and Tanzania, where it is thinly scattered. In breeding plumage the male is mainly black with the top of the head and lower underparts a bright buff, the rump and upper tail coverts streaked with pale buff, and has four thinly elongated straw-colored tail feathers measuring some 7 in. (18 cm). Out of "color," the male and female are similar, being dark buff with darker striations above and plain pale buff below.

The diet is as for the Combassou, except that larger amounts of live food are desirable.

Not often available, the Fischer's Whydah is keenly sought and easy to maintain. It mixes well with other species, but its host species when breeding, the Purple Grenadier, may be considered to be too valuable to be placed with it during the breeding season. It may, however, parasitize other waxbill species. Once established, it is fairly hardy, but it does not like damp or frosty conditions.

A male **Fischer's Whydah** in full dress is also called a Straw-Tailed Whydah.

Golden Song Sparrow

(Auripasser luteus)

Golden Song Sparrow is something of a misnomer for this species, for it is neither golden nor a singer. There must be many people who, having purchased it, were rather disappointed with the result. It is, however, a good avicultural species, mixing well and easy to keep, although it does not do well in a cage.

Ranging from Senegal, through Mali and northern Nigeria, Sudan, and Ethiopia, this canary-like small seed eater is abundant in many parts and so is commonly kept as an aviary species. It is predominantly yellow and chestnut with a brown tail and black wings. The sexes are identified by the female's head and mantle being brown rather than the chestnut of the male.

A fairly willing breeder, it would be more so if true pairs were more frequently obtained. Often birds bought as females turn out to be immature males. A large, untidy nest of grasses is made if a natural site is chosen, but the bird will use a box or basket nest if it is placed in cover. Usually peaceful when breeding, they make a good colony given the opportunity. Live food, seeding grasses, green food, and germinated seeds are required when rearing young; otherwise, they do well on a mixture of small millets and canary seed.

The **Golden Song Sparrow** is rather less golden than its name suggests.

Ease of care (scale 1–10) 1

5 in. (13 cm)

Planted aviary

Some heat required

Good mixer

Quiet

3–5 eggs

12 days incubation

Yellow Bishop

(Euplectes afer)

Also known as the Napolean Weaver, this species is typical of the weaver family, and most others can be treated in the same way. In breeding plumage the male is bright yellow on the forehead, crown, nape, and sides of the neck;

The **Yellow Bishop** is not easy to breed in captivity; it needs the stimulus of a flock.

flanks, breast, and upper tail coverts are a duller yellow, while the lower breast and abdomen are black. The wings and tail are gray-brown. Females and males in eclipse are light brown with darker streaks and paler underparts. In nuptial plumage, the Bishop makes an attractive addition to any collection of similar birds, but like most weavers and sparrows, it cannot be trusted with small fry.

Most weavers are difficult to persuade to breed, and the Yellow Bishop is no exception. It needs the incentive of a sizable group to bring it into condition. A major requirement for breeding success would be considerable amounts of live food added to its usual diet of seeding grasses, mixed millets, and millet spray.

Similar species

Red Bishop
Golden-Backed Bishop
Yellow-Rumped Bishop

Ease of care (scale 1–10) 1

4¾ in. (12 cm)

Planted aviary

Heating unnecessary

May attack smaller birds

Quiet

3–6 eggs

12–14 days incubation

2 Ease of care
(scale 1–10)

5½–8 in.
(14–22 cm)

Cage

Heating
unnecessary

Good
mixer

Quiet

3–6 eggs

14 days
incubation

Canary
(Serinus canaria)

In spite of its many color forms and variations in type, the domestic canary is still regarded in science as the same species as its wild progenitor, the small green and yellow bird found in the Canary Islands. You might think the islands were named the Canaries after the birds, but this is not so: the name comes from the Latin *canis*, dog, for the Romans found the islands overrun with dogs.

Canaries first reached mainland Europe around the 15th century, imported with cargoes of sugar, and at that time they were known as "sugar birds." Kept in cages as tame songbirds, they spread through Italy to Germany where the villagers of the remote Harz Mountains kept and bred them for their song, which was discovered to be learned in some degree and therefore capable of being improved. The first canaries to reach Britain were already bred and known for their continuous rolling song, and became known as "Roller Canaries."

This was effectively the first variety of domesticated canary, and from it has stemmed a vast array of birds bred for their feather pattern, their shape and stance, or their color. Some types are large, such as Lancashire, Yorkshire, and Norwich Plainhead canaries bred for their size and stance, with special color agents added to their food to improve their color. Others, such as the Gloster and Stafford, are bred with a crested form

The color of the **Red-Factor Canary** (opposite) is enhanced by special feeding.

The **Norwich Canary** (below) is bred for shape and feather.

The frosted new type of **Stafford Canary** (above) is becoming more and more popular.

This male green **Border Canary** (above) is bred for shape, not color.

Many **Gloster Corona Canaries** are green or darkly variegated.

which is also found in the Lancashire Coppy and Crested Norwich. The Border and Fife are bred for their shape and feather texture, while the Scotch Fancy and Belgian Fancy are bred for their exaggerated stance. In addition to this, there are varieties bred for the exaggeration of the body feathers into a frilled form, such as the Dutch and Parisian Frill. Of the song canary, there are now three internationally recognized forms: the German Roller Canary, the Belgian Waterslager, and the Spanish Timbrados. A different song canary has been developed in the United States, known as the American Singer, but has yet to be recognized outside the United States.

The song canaries are all required to perform in front of a judge, within a given time, a recognized song of up to 12 parts which, while they may be produced in any order, must be of a particular standard. The judge uses his ears, not his eyes, and judges four birds singing at once – a difficult and unusual task. Type canaries are judged by eye only. They must be clean, bright, healthy, and in the standard cage required for the breed. To produce a bird in good condition on the day, perfect in feather, shape, and deportment, takes breeders many years. Often such birds have taken a lifetime to produce.

Irrespective of their various forms, nearly all canaries require the same basic husbandry when breeding or simply kept for the pleasure of their song. The exception is the competition song canary, which because part of its song is learned, must be kept away from the unwanted influence of other canary songs.

The diet is of mixed seeds, including canary seed, rape, some millet, hemp, niger, and teazel, together with green food in the form of dandelion, chickweed, and lettuce given fresh throughout the year, plus soaked seeds and a rearing food of hard-boiled eggs and biscuit when birds are raising chicks. Many commercial rearing foods are now available.

Canaries may be bred in cages or aviaries, although cage breeding is a must for the serious breeder of exhibition birds; otherwise, important winning lines are never established. As aviary subjects they are good mixers, hardy and undemanding. However, they will quickly destroy

The **Parisian Frill Canary** is bred for its extraordinary feather structure.

any living plants and are best kept in a bare flight. To give my own canaries added enjoyment in an otherwise bare flight, I frequently change the natural perches and in season give them large bunches of seeding grasses in which they play and feed. Often large numbers of young canaries going through their molt will feather-pluck each other quite badly. Giving them something to do in this way frequently overcomes their desire to peck each other until they bleed.

Starlings and Larger Softbills

To anyone other than an aviculturalist, the word "starling" is synonymous with the common European Starling, much maligned city dweller that is now also numerous in America. However, of the 100-plus species of starlings found through the Old World, the vast majority are stunningly colorful iridescent birds. They make wonderful aviary subjects, providing you have space for single-species accommodations, for they are frequently murderous with small birds.

A **Common Mynah**, renowned for its intelligence and tuneful call.

Mynahs vary from the striking Rothschild's Mynah to the best-known talking bird outside the parrot family, the Indian Hill Mynah, famed for its remarkable mimicry. The crows, jays, and magpies also have great attractions: many speak, and all have confidence and make good aviary subjects. The larger black crows need space. Where they may be taken from the wild, they offer the opportunity to seek color mutations. Most of the jays are naturally colorful.

Philippine Glossy Starling

(Aplonis panayensis)

Starlings such as the **Philippine Glossy** are often brilliantly colored.

This glossy black bird, showing iridescent green and purple in good light and with red eyes, is one of a dozen described subspecies found in Burma, Thailand, Vietnam, and various islands through to the Philippines. They are abundant throughout their range and, while not too often available, are a popular avicultural species. It is difficult to obtain a true pair, however, for the sexes are alike.

Easily managed, although often nervous to start with, they can be bred if given the right conditions. Hole nest boxes are the best, and plenty of live food is required in the form of crickets, locusts, and mealworms. Outside the breeding season they are mainly fruit eaters, but will accept commercial insectivorous mixture.

Most starlings are potentially aggressive at all times of the year and need to be watched, but breeding pairs should be housed separately as a matter of course. Generally hardy after acclimatization, they should be given frost-free roosting quarters, but overwinter well.

Similar species

Purple Glossy Starling
Green Glossy Starling

Ease of care (scale 1–10) 3

9 in. (23 cm)

Planted aviary

Some heat required

Keep alone or as pair

Quiet

3–5 eggs

14 days incubation

Long-Tailed Glossy Starling

(Lamprotornis caudatus)

Widely distributed throughout Africa, its populations are often quite localized, which makes it less readily available. It is, however, a very colorful and worthwhile avicultural species. Bronze green on the head with an iridescent green body, it has violet flanks and a purple and blue tail. Although the sexes are alike, the female is smaller, which makes the species less difficult to sex than other starlings. The species should be treated as the Philippine Starling, although it is less happy with fruit.

The **Long-Tailed Glossy Starling** is a stunning bird in good light.

Ease of care (scale 1–10) 3

24 in. (60 cm)

Planted aviary

Some heat required

Keep alone or as pair

Quiet

2–6 eggs

14–15 days incubation

Ease of care
(scale 1–10)
3

 7¾ in.
(20 cm)

 Planted
aviary

 Heating
unnecessary

 May attack
smaller birds

 Quiet

 2–6 eggs

 14–15 days
incubation

Spreo Starling

(Spreo superbus)

The **Spreo Starling** is quite beautiful and readily available.

This species is the most widely kept of all the starlings, as it is easy to manage and quite hardy. Also known as the Superb Starling, its head, nape, and throat are black, the neck and breast iridescent blue, with metallic green wings and mantle, spotted with sooty black. A fine white line divides the blue breast from the chestnut underparts. The tail is black.

Spreos are widespread and abundant in Ethiopia, Somalia, Uganda, and Kenya, and very readily available. They breed very well in captivity, using a deep nest box, but need plenty of live food in the form of crickets, locusts, mealworms, etc., in addition to insectivorous food with some fruit and berries. This confident species does well in outdoor flights provided the roost is frost-free. It can become very tame and outside the breeding season is an excellent mixer.

Similar species

**Emerald Starling
Chestnut Bellied Starling
Malabar Starling**

 Ease of care
(scale 1–10)
4

 7 in.
(18 cm)

 Planted
aviary

 Heating
essential

 May attack
smaller birds

 Quiet

 2–3 eggs

15 days
incubation

Amethyst Starling

(Cinnyricinclus leucogaster)

Also known as the Violet Starling, this bird is an avicultural gem. The head and the whole of the upper surface is a brilliant iridescent violet, while the underside is white. The reflective plumage shines green, purple, and bronze according to the light. Also, there is no problem with sexing as the female, if you are lucky enough to find one, is streaked brown above and buff below.

There are good populations across Central Africa, Ethiopia, and the Sudan. While importation is patchy, once the bird is obtained, it makes an easily managed subject, although breeding is not often recorded.

Generally more peaceful than many of the other starlings, they make good subjects for a mixed collection, but they are not hardy in winter and must have a frost-free environment.

The beautiful coloring of the male **Amethyst Starling** is wonderfully reflective.

Ease of care
(scale 1–10)

14 in.
(35 cm)

Planted
aviary

Heating
essential

Keep alone
or as pair

Quiet

2–6 eggs

14–15 days
incubation

Royal Starling

(Cosmopsarus regius)

The **Royal Starling** is probably the most sought after of the exotic starlings.

Rarely available and consequently expensive, the Royal Starling is the most sought and highly regarded of the African starlings. The head and nape are metallic green, the mantle black, and wings iridescent violet; yellow underparts and a bronze and greenish blue tail make this an altogether striking bird.

I have found some individuals quite confident once settled in, while others have been nervous and highly strung. They quickly become tame. As with most starlings, the sexes are alike. Generally omnivorous, they enjoy berries and fruits, ground meat, a commercial insect mixture and, of course, live food, particularly when breeding.

Hole nesters in the wild, Royal Starlings prefer a deep nest box, which they line with roots and fibers. I have found them stripping honeysuckle bark when nesting, and tearing roots from grass sods (turves) put into the aviary as a source of insects.

Royal Starlings are not wonderfully hardy, and frost-free quarters are a must over winter, while outdoor flights may be used to advantage during summer months.

Ease of care (scale 1–10)

 8½ in. (22 cm)

 Planted aviary

 Heating unnecessary

 Keep alone or as pair

 Quiet

 4–5 eggs

 16 days incubation

Common Starling

(Sturnus vulgaris)

The **Common Starling** is a fascinating species to keep as an aviary or pet bird.

This species, so well known for its habit of flocking in vast numbers during the winter, raiding bird tables and driving off weaker birds, is the typical bird success story. Taken from Europe to America, it has become a ubiquitous city dweller, frequently dirty and argumentative. However, cleaned up and given aviary space, and a lot of patience, this bird will turn into a gleaming iridescent black, bronze, green, and blue charmer. One of the few species in the British Isles that may be taken from the wild at any time, it has a lot to offer. Anyone who has seen some of the stunning mutations could hardly fail to agree.

Because a species is common, it is often disregarded. The Starling is one of these, and more effort should be put into breeding it.

A diet of puppy meal, insectivorous mixture, cooked peas, brown bread, and milk, together with plenty of live food, will bring a Starling into high condition. The species is surprisingly difficult to breed. It needs huge amounts of live food if you are to succeed. Hand-raised birds are often best. They become very tame and can be flown at liberty if the surroundings permit. Although I have not tried personally, I would think this a most rewarding exercise.

Rothschild's Starling

(Leucopsar rothschild)

Often called the Bali Mynah or Bali Starling, this species is seriously endangered in the wild. Rothschild's Starling is found only on the island of Bali. It is a white bird, with black wingtips and a black terminal band to the tail; a long white crest sweeps back over the shoulders, and the area of bare skin on the face is bright blue. The sexes are similar, except that the female carries a smaller crest. In spite of its endangered status, there are now good captive populations. However, breeders are urged to register their stock with the international stud book.

A good diet of commercial insect food with chopped beef heart, hard-boiled egg, and vast quantities of crickets, locusts, and mealworms when breeding is required. Some compatible pairs breed extraordinarily well, others not at all. They are best kept as a single species. Reasonably hardy, they do need frost-free winter quarters.

Rothschild's Starling is rare, but careful breeding has saved it from extinction.

Ease of care (scale 1–10) 3

10 in. (25 cm)

Planted aviary

Some heat required

Keep alone or as pair

Quiet

3–4 eggs

14–16 days incubation

Common Mynah

(Acridothere tristis)

The **Common Mynah** is an intelligent and amusing species.

With a black head, chin, and throat, a dark brown back, white wing patch, and light brown to white underparts, an orange bill, and yellow legs, this species is not one of the more colorful. Found naturally throughout India, eastward to China and Sri Lanka, it has also been introduced into Australia, New Zealand, South Africa, and Hawaii.

The Common Mynah is an intelligent and amusing species, readily available. True pairs, which are often difficult to determine, are free breeding. The species enjoys a good mixed diet of commercial insect food, ground raw meat, fruit and berries, with abundant live food when rearing chicks. Completely hardy, the bird can be mixed with similar-sized species unless breeding, when single accommodations are a must. The calls are quite loud, but pleasant.

Similar species

Pagoda Mynah

Ease of care (scale 1–10) 1

9½ in. (24 cm)

Planted aviary

Heating unnecessary

Keep alone or as pair

Noisy at times

3–5 eggs

15 days incubation

Ease of care (scale 1–10) — 2

14 in. (36 cm)

Cage

Some heat required

Keep alone or as pair

Noisy at times

2–3 eggs

16 days incubation

Greater Hill Mynah

(Gracula r. religiosa)

The Greater Hill Mynah is one of ten subspecies of the Southern Grackle, and hails from Malaysia, Borneo, Java, and Sumatra. It is a glossy black with a white patch on the wing, orange beak, and yellow legs, with a bare swattle of yellow skin on the sides of the head. At times, this species has been overcollected for the pet trade, mainly because its ability to talk so well has made it a popular cage bird.

As a pet bird it is best obtained while still gaping for food, which will guarantee its juvenile status. This is important, since adult birds will not learn to talk, nor add to an existing vocabulary. Any words or phrases not included in the first year will not normally ever be learned. If you keep a Mynah as a talking pet, beware of what you teach it to say. My mother taught a pet Mynah to say "Where's Graham? Gone to Germany!" when I was posted there with the army in 1957. He

The **Greater Hill Mynah** is a talking bird of great ability.

continued to say it for the next 15 years. As an aviary species, it is fairly hardy but does require frost-free housing over winter. Captive breeding has been recorded with a number of subspecies, but I do not think this is the case with the Greater. Certainly it would require single accommodations and plenty of live food.

Similar species

Lesser Hill Mynah

Ease of care (scale 1–10) — 2

12 in. (30 cm)

Planted aviary

Heating unnecessary

Keep alone or as pair

Noisy at times

3–5 eggs

17 days incubation

European Jay

(Garrulus glandarius)

The European Jay is shy and restless in the wild, where it is considered a pest species. As an aviary subject, it is often tame and confiding. With blue eyes, binocular vision, and the ability to talk, it makes a very interesting subject as a single species. While not as colorful as the tropical jays, the European is full of color: it is a vivaceous brown above with chin, throat, and belly white, the wings black, white, and chestnut, and an erectile black and white crest. Its black, blue, and white barred wing coverts have been used for hat decoration and for fishing flies. The sexes are alike.

If breeding, the birds require seclusion and a good diet of mixed puppy meal and insectivorous food. Live food must be provided, and stepped up long before nesting takes place. Ground raw meat and small dead mice (pinkies) or dead day-old chicks are a welcome addition, as are nuts and berries. Jays are now credited with the planting of

The shy, woodland **European Jay** can become tame and will also learn to talk.

many oak trees, with individual birds burying hundreds of acorns each fall. The nest is a see-through affair of twigs and roots, and it is best to provide a number of alternative sites in the form of wire platforms or open boxes.

Red-Billed Blue Magpie

(Urocissa erythrorhyncha)

The Himalayas, northern India, and Indochina are home to this popular species. Gray blue and brown above, lilac and white below with white tips to most of the main wing feathers, it has a black, blue, and white head and nape, and a long 16-in. (40-cm) graduated magpie tail of mauve tipped with black and white. The bill from which it takes its name is bright red.

This bird needs lots of space and plenty of natural cover. Easy to manage and fairly free-breeding on an open box or wire shelf, it must have lots of live food in addition to the usual mix of predatory foods and ground raw meat. Also freely taken are small rats and mice, including pinkies and day-old chicks. If imported, the Blue Magpie must be in good plumage before it is trusted to outside weather conditions, but once acclimatized it can be quite hardy. An inveterate

The **Red-Billed Blue Magpie** needs lots of room to keep in good condition.

thief of eggs and chicks, this active and intelligent bird is best housed as a single-species pair. Single birds will live with larger birds, but those of equal size or smaller are in for a hard time.

Similar species

Green Hunting Cissa
Azure-Winged Magpie

Ease of care (scale 1–10)

26 in. (65 cm)

Planted aviary

Heating unnecessary

Keep alone or as pair

Noisy at times

3–5 eggs

17 days incubation

Green Jay

(Cyanocorax yncas)

The **Green Jay** is a good subject for a large aviary.

Found in Central America, Mexico, southern Texas down through Venezuela, Ecuador, and Peru, this is a wide-ranging and colorful species. The forehead and cheek patches and a small patch above the eye are bright cobalt blue, set off by a black beak, sides of the head, throat, and upper breast. The crown and nape are white, blue, and yellow, while the upper surface of the wing is bright green, with a tail of green, blue, and yellow. There are 12 or 13 subspecies that have considerable variation in plumage. It does well on a diet similar to that of the European Jay.

A good avicultural subject, it requires a large aviary in which to show itself at its best. It is easily managed, but needs plenty of cover. An open nest box or a nest platform should be provided if you hope to breed the species as, like the European Jay, the Green Jay builds a very flimsy nest. Unless plenty of live food is given, it is not unusual for this bird to eat its young chicks. The bird is active and noisy, and does not like cold, damp conditions or close confinement. Frost-free winter quarters are essential.

Similar species

Plush-Crested Jay

Ease of care (scale 1–10)

12 in. (30 cm)

Planted aviary

Some heat required

Keep alone or as pair

Noisy at times

3–5 eggs

18 days incubation

Ease of care
(scale 1–10)

20 in.
(50 cm)

Bare
aviary

Heating
unnecessary

Keep alone
or as pair

Noisy
at times

4–6 eggs

21 days
incubation

Magpie

(Pica pica)

The ubiquitous Magpie is almost too well known to need description. The head, nape, mantle, and breast are glossy black, while the lower breast, underparts, parts of the primary feathers, and scapulars are white. The tail is black, as are the legs, feet, and bill. There is a yellow-billed form found in California. The sexes are alike. An occasional aviary subject, the Magpie is a pest species over most of its range and may be taken freely from the wild, allowing the aviculturalist to try for color mutations. I have seen wild specimens in cinnamon, white, and silver.

It is very hardy, active and entertaining, can be taught to speak, and will breed fairly readily. The diet can be almost anything, it seems, for I have found little remotely edible that will not be taken with gusto: soaked puppy meal, leftovers from the kitchen (both meat and vegetables), live food, and dead day-old chicks.

The pesky **Magpie** makes a good aviary bird, and pet birds can be kept at liberty.

Sturdy twigs are used to build a dome nest. Although the aviary needs to be quite bare, for the birds are destructive, they will build in an open-fronted box or on a wire platform if it is secluded.

Ease of care
(scale 1–10)

12 in.
(30 cm)

Cage

Heating
unnecessary

Keep alone
or as pair

Quiet

3–4 eggs

16 days
incubation

Jackdaw

(Corvus monedula)

Smaller than most of its corvine cousins, the Jackdaw is a glossy black bird with a gray head, black feet and bill, and a gray ring around the eye. It is gregarious, intelligent, and amusing. It is also destructive and a thief. Most of the birds I have kept or known have been free-flying hand-reared birds, which become very demanding and inquisitive, while prepared to steal anything bright that attracts attention, much more so than the famous "thieving magpie." As a boy walking to school I, like most of my friends, had a tame Jackdaw or Crow that followed us, drove the teachers to distraction, and waited on the school fence for our journey home.

As an aviary subject, it is quite rare, although it has much to commend it, but I suspect any breeding success would require a small colony to be established. It is very insectivorous; although, like the Magpie, it will do well on a varied diet.

The small **Jackdaw** is an interesting species and should be more widely kept.

26–28 in. (65–70 cm)

Bare aviary

Heating unnecessary

Keep alone or as pair

Noisy at times

4–6 eggs

21 days incubation

Raven

(Corvus corax)

Ravens have been kept at the Tower of London for centuries.

The description of this widespread species can be summed up briefly: a large, glossy black bird with a heavy black bill. The Raven is found throughout Europe, America, and Asia in cold and inhospitable areas, often well away from human habitation. It is well known in Britain as the bird kept at the Tower of London to guarantee the continuation of the realm, but in spite of many hundreds of years of captivity, only recently has the bird bred there. It is a large, grave, and sedate bird, with great character. Highly sought after, it is listed as endangered and is therefore difficult to obtain. Of the many birds I am asked to find for potential keepers, this is one of the most popular. Its croaking call is loud, deep, and uttered with some force.

Living in open places, existing mainly on carrion and not averse to killing small birds or weak lambs, it is an opportunist omnivore. The bird needs space, with plenty of live food and fresh meat, including rodents, day-old chicks, and rabbits. To breed this species, it would be best to provide a deep shelf running across the rear of an aviary, filled with a layer of sand, to simulate the natural rock faces on which it likes to build its large and untidy stick nest.

Dealing with Disease

If ever there was a specter at the feast in aviculture, it is the threat of disease occurring in your stock. Keepers often feel that consulting a vet in an attempt to cure small birds is throwing good money after bad, and here I have certainly been as skeptical as most. At one time, I was the proud owner of a high quality competition stud of Roller Canaries. An unknown disease hit my birds, and in spite of immediate veterinary involvement, several postmortem examinations, and months spent trying to resolve the problem, my breeding group of 48 birds was reduced to three.

Nail clippers and a fine artist's brush

The main difficulty is that many small birds show no symptoms until they are past the point of no return, so that by the time you realize they are sick, it is often too late to treat them. Sometimes, too, symptoms are so general as to make instant diagnosis impossible. However, in recent years advances have been made in the area of small bird disease, and more vets are taking an interest in avian medicine. This especially applies to parrots and birds of prey, probably because of the dramatic rise in the number of keepers and the birds' high value, which encourages keepers to seek medical help.

Good stockmanship and an eye for detail are important. A good keeper should know all his birds and be aware of any change in behavior long before any other observer notices a thing. Knowing and studying your birds pays dividends.

If disease appears in one bird, isolate it immediately. Do not lose one, then seek help; seek help at once. You may not save the first one, but if an infection is about to sweep through your stock, treatment may save the rest. Bacterial infections may be treatable; viral infections generally are not. You must stop disease at the source. When you buy new birds, quarantine them as a matter of course. However, the stress of quarantine often causes masked problems to flare quickly out of control. With both parrots and pigeons, the highly

Anti-mite spray and antiseptic cream

infectious Newcastle disease (fowl pest), often appears in newly acquired birds. In birds of prey, especially Goshawks, *Aspergillus* infection appears to be endemic in all populations and if the birds are stressed, the disease surfaces and it is a fight to keep any bird alive long enough to treat it.

Problems occur when you least expect them, and often at the most inconvenient times. It helps, therefore, if you are well prepared and able to administer first aid, without having to move to full crisis management. Many sick birds that would otherwise be lost have been saved by having the basics of first aid handy. Warmth, quiet, and rest will go a long way toward achieving this. Over the years I have been involved in the rescue and rehabilitation of a great many wild creatures, both birds and mammals. A warm, dark place may often be all a canary needs, and a cardboard box of the right size can be one of your best medicines. If the next stage of treatment involves a journey to the vet, I find it helps to have a piece of carpet in the bottom of the box, which stops the bird from sliding backward and forward with every movement on the journey.

If heat is required, I use a ceramic light heater, the type used by pig farmers to keep piglets warm. If an ordinary bulb is splashed with water, it will explode. The heavy ceramic lamps are made to avoid this problem, and also do not give off light, so that the patient remains in the comfort of darkness. Other requirements for home treatment include fine artist's brushes, nail clippers, good-quality forceps, antiseptic cream, wound powder, and glucose powder.

Glucose powder

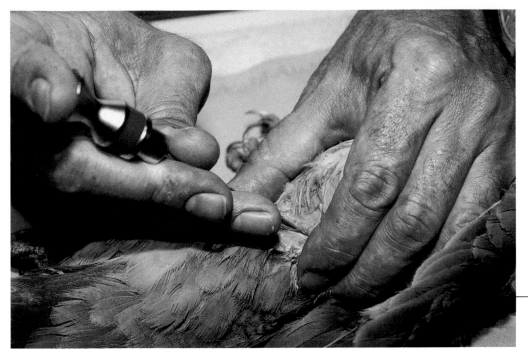

Dehydration is often a real problem during the early stages of treatment, especially in cases of diarrhea or heavy bleeding, and liquid solutions such as glucose and saline may be required to keep the patients well hydrated. There are now several commercial rehydration solutions available, one of which should be included in your medicine chest.

Injuries that involve bleeding should always be treated by your vet, especially if there is internal bleeding. Both will send a bird into shock, and prompt first aid is needed for a bleeding wound. Apply pressure at the site and then use a clean gauze bandage, followed by a tight binding. Before covering any open wound, make sure that it is clean, using a mild antiseptic, and clip away any feathers sticking into the wound.

Broken limbs must be immobilized. Wing and thigh breaks should be taped close to the body. Broken lower leg joints must be handled with great care. Unless secured gently but firmly, such a break will result in the loss of the limb.

One common condition that usually responds to gentle heat and rest is egg binding. When hens are about to begin laying, they frequently lapse into a trance-like state known as egg lethargy. Should this reach the stage where a hen is overdue to lay after starting her clutch and is clearly distressed, to the degree that she is resting on the cage or aviary floor, you should suspect egg binding and react accordingly. The bird should be handled very carefully; rough handling may break the egg inside her, which is fatal. Gently lubricate the cloaca with warm olive oil on a soft paint-brush, and leave the bird to recover in a warm place. Closely monitor the bird's condition, and if after 24 hours the egg is not expelled, seek further help. Occasionally the bird may suffer a prolapse, which needs expert veterinary help, but generally the hen will recover, complete her clutch, and continue breeding without further problems.

Once the initial first aid is over and treatment has begun, you may be required to give drugs for some time. If the bird needs to be kept still, warm, and in the dark, you will certainly need to administer fluids several times a day. Sick birds will often refuse to drink in any quantity, and as most drugs not administered by injection are given in water, a stomach tube is a valuable tool.

Gauze bandage and surgical tape

Although you may encounter diseases that are brought into your stock by newly purchased birds, and which you can counter by giving new stock a period of quarantine, diseases may also come from the droppings of wild birds perching on an open aviary. Pseudotuberculosis is one such disease that is very difficult to eradicate. There is no treatment, but prevention is possible; cover your aviary.

Avian pox, spread by mosquitoes, is common in the United States, though less so in Britain. Canaries are among the worst affected, and many keepers cover their outside flights with mosquito nets to help alleviate the problem. There is no treatment, but should the bird recover, it will be immune for the rest of its life.

Enteritis, one of the most prevalent problems with birds, is caused by various bacteria. The dreaded "Going Light" syndrome is a form of enteritis; much has been written on this subject and many years devoted to finding a cure. It occurs in young birds recently fledged, particularly greenfinches and canaries, and older birds suffering from a bad molt. The birds are seen at the feeding station constantly, fluffed up and lethargic. They seem simply to waste away, with death following a protracted illness in older birds, but coming within days for fledglings. The birds are as thin and light as thistledown at the end.

I have never been an enthusiastic user of many of the so-called preventative medicines now commonly available to bird keepers. A chest packed full of vitamin supplements and various oils and tinctures is generally unnecessary if you feed a sensible, balanced diet. However, in recent years I have come to use a probiotic additive, which has entirely prevented enteritis among my small birds. Recently, I saved a very sick peregrine falcon by using probiotic fluids fed straight into the crop by tube, followed when he began to eat by a daily dose of powder inside his diet of quail and rats.

A number of bird diseases are zoonoses – that is, they can be passed on to humans. These include psittacosis, pseudotuberculosis, avian tuberculosis, and *salmonella* food poisoning. While they are relatively uncommon, you should be on your guard. Treatment of the affected birds frequently prevents human infection, but equally often this fails. Such diseases passed to very young or old people may even be fatal. Because of the risks, many veterinarians will only treat rare or valuable birds with these diseases.

Any discussion of disease, no matter how brief, tends to leave you worried about all the dreadful and incurable ailments that are going to affect your

AVIAN DISEASES

Newcastle Disease
A viral disease, clinical signs are head twisting and lack of coordination.

Feather Plucking
Self-plucking is a clear sign of stress, often due to overbreeding in females.

Avian Pox
Scales and lesions appear around the beak, eyes, and on the feet.

Enteritis
Wet feathers around the vent indicate enteritis, needing rapid treatment.

birds. However, all is not gloom, for many problems are avoidable and treatable should they occur. These include most of the parasitic infections, both from ectoparasites, which live on the host, and from endoparasites, which live inside the host.

Most of the ectoparasites – mites, lice, and fleas – may be quickly killed with an insecticidal spray specially formulated to deal with them. Red mite is one of the most perennial, living in the environment during the day and feeding on the host at night. Nesting canaries may be dreadfully debilitated and even killed by a major red mite infection; here the mites live in the nest material.

Endoparasites – worms and flukes – have a complex and nauseating life cycle. Gapeworms, tapeworms, and flukes may be passed through the droppings of wild birds, or as the larvae inhabiting earthworms. Happily, they, too, can be treated simply today by a number of drugs available from your vet, or even sold over the counter at a good pet store.

Problems with the parrot family that at first may be thought to be caused by ectoparasites include various feather conditions. Feather plucking, sometimes to the extent where a bird resembles an oven-ready chicken, still has to be traced to a specific cause, but is mostly a habit akin to nail biting that stems from boredom, stress, overly dry conditions, or a combination of all three. There is, however, a serious feather condition that is spreading rapidly throughout the captive parrot population: psittacine beak and feather disease. In spite of extensive research, no cure has yet been found.

Feather problems are not restricted to parrots, and hereditary conditions exist in various types of canaries. Norwich and Gloster Canaries suffer from feather cysts, known as "lumps," which can generally be traced to inbreeding of buff-feathered stock (buff being a feather type in which the feathers become unusually bulky). The usual mating of type canaries is yellow to buff, yellow feather types producing a finer, sleeker bird with less material in the individual feathers. Constant double-buff mating brings the increased feather volume, but ultimately feather cysts.

You do not need to be a trained veterinary surgeon to spot and deal with most of the more usual avian problems. It always helps to practice good stockmanship. Know your birds in their various moods, and if their behavior changes unexpectedly, seek expert help at once.

Psittacosis (PBFD)
A bacterial disease, symptoms include nasal discharge and enteritis.

Ticks
Ticks land on the bird and swell up as they suck the blood from their host.

Scaly Face
Mites multiply around the eyes and base of the beak, producing scales.

Overgrown Beak
Advanced cases of scaly face can prevent birds from trimming their beaks.

Avicultural terms

Albinism

Lack of pigment produces a bird with pure white feathers, pink eyes, and pale feet, claws, and beak. Albino chicks produced by parents not themselves albino are invariably female. Partial albinism occurs frequently, most noticeably in dark-colored birds such as European blackbirds where patches of white feathers produce a pied effect.

Buff

A color form related to feather structure. Buff-feathered birds appear to have more bulk due to additional filament in the feathers. Show breeders pair buff birds together to produce longer, bulkier feathered birds, typically budgerigars and canaries. Regular use of double-buffing results in feather cysts, as often seen in Norwich canaries. Buff birds appear to have a slight frosting effect on the feather tips. (*see also* Yellow)

Cere

The soft tissue at the base of the bill of many species, typically parrots and birds of prey, which contains the nostrils.

Close-ringing

A closed circular ring (that is, one with no break in it) is placed on the leg of a chick while it is small. As the bird grows, the ring fits snugly and cannot slip off; it can only be removed by cutting. Close-ringing is done either to comply with the law, or to identify the bird for competition purposes.

Color food

A variety of methods of color feeding to produce intensity of color are now available in the form of liquids that are added to the water, or dry foods added to a soft food mixture. Color food is generally used to add orange or red color to the birds' plumage, either to retain the natural red series that many birds lose in captivity, or to enhance the depth of color in show birds, such as red-factor canaries.

Condition seed

A mix of high protein seeds given sparingly that help the bird during periods of stress, such as when breeding, molting, or showing. Given too frequently, they produce the opposite effect.

Coping

The trimming of beaks and claws that have become overgrown.

Coverts

The feathers that cover the undersides of the longer, main feathers of a bird's wings or tail.

Egg bound

A potentially serious condition in which the hen bird is unable to produce an egg at the appointed time. This condition is obvious, even to the novice. The bird is clearly in distress, fluffed, and making frequent visits to the nest. Warmth and a steam bath, and gentle oiling of the vent with a small brush dipped in olive oil, may resolve the problem, but great care must be taken not to break the egg inside the bird, which will result in death.

Hardbills

A term most often applied to seed-eating birds that do not rely on insect food, except when rearing young.

Hybrid

A bird produced from mating two separate species. They are frequently infertile.

Imprinting

This applies particularly to birds of prey. When very young, they naturally imprint on their parents. Birds reared by hand imprint on the person rearing them and become very tame. However, such birds are incapable of natural reproduction, responding only to their human keeper, and therefore require artificial insemination. Some imprinted birds can be aggressive.

Intermewed

A term used by falconers to describe a hawk or falcon that has been through a molt.

Going light

A condition in which birds rapidly lose weight and die, believed to be due to a build-up of the gut bacteria *E. coli*. It can be controlled by regular use of a probiotic. In small birds, once the disease has a grip there is little chance of a reversal.

Lutino

An albinistic form in which, instead of white, the feathers are buttercup yellow. This occurs in green birds whose feathers are based on a yellow ground color, such as green series budgerigars.

Liberty birds

Those species that may be allowed complete freedom, yet will stay in or around the property. Peafowl, pigeons, and some parrots will do well at complete liberty. Others, such as firefinches, need the protection of an aviary and shelter at night.

Molt

The change of feathers that normally occurs once each year. This can be a time of stress, particularly for many small birds.

Night-fright

Diurnal birds, when disturbed at night, may panic and explode into flight. Unable to see, they often injure and sometimes kill themselves by striking the aviary roof. Such frights are usually attributed to night prowlers, such as cats, mice, or owls.

Parasitic species

Birds that lay their eggs in the nests of others. Most of the species of whydah use small seed eaters as hosts for their offspring, making them difficult to breed in captivity.

Pinioning

The surgical removal of part of one wing at the wrist joint, typically carried out with young ducklings and goslings to prevent birds otherwise at liberty from flying away.

Probiotic

A powdered culture of micro-organisms *(Enteroccus faecium)* designed as a feeding supplement to aid the establishment of a healthy gut flora, thus overcoming many digestive tract problems. Many birds suffer from such intestinal problems, either when just fledging or at other times of stress, such as during breeding. Probiotics are widely recognized as the way to overcome this potential problem.

Red factor

This term is applied strictly to a hybridized form of canary, crossbred to a red-hooded siskin to add a red gene to the canary. Red-factor canaries are now well established, some achieving the original aim of producing bright red canaries.

Softbills

This term is difficult to describe. Generally, it refers to insect-eating species, which feed their chicks by food carried in the bill rather than food carried in the crop and regurgitated.

Soft food

A mixture of hard-boiled egg and biscuit meal that is fed to many birds when rearing chicks.

Type birds

Varieties of birds, usually canaries, that are bred for their shape and general conformation: long, slim birds such as the Yorkshire canary; large, heavily feathered birds such as the Norwich canary; or diminutive, rounded birds such as the Fife fancy canary.

Unflighted

A term describing young birds that have molted their nest feathers but still retain the flight and tail feathers produced in the nest.

Yellow

A form of feather structure where the color is bright and clear. It produces birds that are slimmer than their buff counterparts. Most breeders try to mate buff-to-yellow to maintain quality of feather. (*see also* Buff)

Aviary plants

Chamaecyparis

There are many varieties of cypress, which are available in colored forms from dark green to pale gray, yellow, and blue. It forms a dense bush or tree with fresh growth on the outermost tips of the plant, and a dry dense interior, ideal for nesting birds. *(type: evergreen)*

Clematis montana

A rapidly growing plant that will quickly produce thick cover. Bearing a mass of small white flowers in spring, it is an exceedingly vigorous plant and needs regular pruning. Because the flowers are borne on the previous year's growth, it is best pruned after flowering. *(type: perennial climber)*

Clematis jackmanii

This is the most popular of the species, with large, showy flowers. Grown either on the outside of an aviary to add color, or on the inside up a post, it is not so vigorous as the montana and is best left unpruned if you wish to use it as cover. The flowers appear on the new growth and for best results the plant should be pruned almost to the ground. *(type: perennial climber)*

Cotoneaster conspicuus v. decorus

A prostrate variety will form a bank of dark green foliage with small white scented flowers, attracting bees and other insects in spring. *(type: evergreen)*

Crataegus monogyna

Clipped as a hedge and planted close together, the hawthorn will form an impenetrable barrier with good nesting sites and edible fruits much loved by thrushes in winter after the frosty weather is over. *(type: plant with edible berries)*

Humulus japonica

The annual hop, sown from seed each year, will rapidly cover a post, giving good cover and attracting insects galore. There is also a type with variegated leaves. *(type: annual climber)*

Ipomea

The morning glory has large blue or white flowers that close in the afternoon. It is best grown in small pots and then planted outside once all danger of frost has passed. *(type: annual climber)*

Jasmine officinale

The summer flowering jasmine is not strictly a climbing plant, but is grown for best effect against a wall or support. Its white flowers, produced in summer, are highly scented. *(type: perennial climber)*

Jasmine nudiflorum

The winter flowering jasmine has bright yellow flowers, produced from October to March on bare green branches, which add color during the dull winter months. *(type: perennial climber)*

Lathyrus odoratus

The sweet pea is available in a huge variety of colors and gives a wonderful display on the outside of an aviary. Seedlings need protection from pecking birds. *(type: annual climber)*

Lathyrus officialnalis

The perennial pea, which will grow fresh each year on the wire of an aviary, produces purple flowers throughout the summer months. It will die back during the winter months, so pruning is unnecessary. *(type: perennial climber)*

Lonicera

There are many species and varieties of honeysuckle. It produces vigorous growth and scented flowers in various shades of pink, cream, and red, which in some cases produce berries appreciated by your birds. Some, such as *frangrantissima*, will flower in winter. *(type: perennial climber)*

Mahonia

The Oregon grape will form a dense shrub six feet (1.8 m) high under the most adverse conditions. It is a useful plant in shaded areas. *(type: evergreen)*

Phaseolus multiflorus

The humble and useful runner bean can be grown either on the aviary wire or on a wigwam of sticks within to produce attractive and useful cover for small birds, together with a good insect population. *(type: annual climber)*

Polygonum baldschunicum

Once established this plant is difficult to control, but given ruthless pruning it provides wonderful cover for breeding birds, and encourages insects. It can produce 30 feet (9 m) of growth in one summer with ease. *(type: perennial climber)*

Pyracantha coccina

Firethorn is a strong growing shrub that may be trained against a wall, giving thorny protection to the inmates of the aviary. Its bright red berries are much appreciated by thrushes and bullfinches, as are the numerous insects it attracts. It is also useful as a perimeter hedge to discourage unwanted intruders in your backyard. *(type: evergreen)*

Rosa canina

The dog rose produces white flowers in spring and early summer, which are followed by bright red fruit in the fall. *(type: plant with edible berries)*

Rubus fruiticosus

The popular blackberry is extremely vigorous and provides cover, insect food, and berries in season. It needs to be cut back hard in winter. Where branches touch the ground, new roots will form. *(type: plant with edible berries)*

Sambucus nigra

The elderberry will grow anywhere, often self-seeding in the most unlikely places. Its flowers attract many insects and its dark luscious fruits are real favorites. *(type: plant with edible berries)*

Symphoicarpus albus

The snowberry produces white berries, borne on the tips of the new growth, much favored by pheasants. *(type: plant with edible berries)*

Birds unsuited to caged life

Although I have indicated the ideal environment for the various birds described in this book, most may be kept safely in either cage or aviary. For breeding success, it is usually better to aim for an aviary. The exceptions to this rule are exhibition birds, where the cage-breeding regime allows for controlled breeding and certain knowledge of parentage. However, the following birds do not normally settle to caged life and are therefore best avoided if cages are your only option.

All Ducks and Geese
All Birds of Prey
Luzon Bleeding-Heart Pigeon
Reeves Pheasant
Roulroul Partridge
Monal Pheasant
Siamese Fireback Pheasant
Golden Pheasant
Silver Pheasant
Common Peafowl
Palm Cockatoo

Indian Ring-Necked Parakeet
Kookaburra
Red-Faced Mousebird
All Touraco
Blue-Crowned Motmot
Red-Billed Hornbill
White-Crested Laughing Thrush
Green Jay
Red-Billed Blue Magpie
Magpie
Raven

Index

Italic numbers refer to illustrations.
Bold numbers refer to main entries for birds, which include illustrations.

A

Acanthis flammea (Linnet) **128**
Accipter nisus (Sparrowhawk) **30**
Acridothere tristis (Common Mynah) **143**
African Grey Parrot 17, 56, **76**, 88
African Silverbill **123**
Agapornis roseicollis (Peach-Faced Lovebird) **77**
Aidemosyne modesta (Cherry Finch) **123**
Aix galericulata (Mandarin Duck) **23**
Alexandrine Parakeet **78**
Amadina fasciata (Cut-Throat Finch) **125**
Amandava amandava (Red Avadavat) **118**
Amandava subflava (Golden-Breasted Waxbill) **119**
Amazona aestiva (Blue-Fronted Amazon Parrot) **88**
Amazona albifrons (White-Fronted Amazon Parrot) **87**
Amazona o. tresmariae (Double Yellow-Headed Amazon) **89**
American Kestrel **32**
American Singer Canary 137
Amethyst Starling **140**
Anas penelope (European Wigeon) **23**
Anus platyrhynchos laysanensis (Laysan Teal) **24**
Aplonis panayensis (Philippine Glossy Starling) **139**
Ara ararauna (Blue and Gold Macaw) **80**
Ara chloroptera (Green-Winged Macaw) **81**
Ara macao (Scarlet Macaw) **81**
Ara manilata (Red-Bellied Macaw) **82**
Ara militaris (Military Macaw) **82**
Ara n. nobilis (Hahn's Macaw) **83**
Aratinga solstitialis (Sun Conure) **83**
Argus Pheasant 46
artificial incubation 17, *17*
Asio otis (Long-Eared Owl) **39**
Aspergillus infection 148
Athene cunicular (Burrowing Owl) **38**
Athene noctua (Little Owl) **36**
Auripasser luteus (Golden Song Sparrow) **133**
avian pox 150, *150*
avian tuberculosis 150
aviaries 8–9, *8*, 12–13, 28–9, 57, 92–3
    skylight/seclusion 29, 30
Aythya fuligula (Tufted Duck) **24**

B

Bali Mynah (Bali Starling) *see* Rothschild's Starling
Barn Owl **36**
Barraband Parakeet **66**
bathing 10–11
Bay-Winged Hawk *see* Harris Hawk
beak, overgrown *151*
Belgian Fancy Canary 137
Belgian Waterslager Canary 137
Bengal Eagle Owl **35**
Bengalese Mannikin **124**
bird rooms 9, *9*, 11
birds of prey 16, 17, **30–39**
    food 14–15, 29
    law 28
    nest sites 29
    and poison 11–12
    special conditions 28–9
Black East Indie Duck **26**
Black Palm Cockatoo 56
Black-Headed Caique **86**
Blue and Gold Macaw **80**
Blue Quail *see* Scaled Quail
Blue Streaked Lory **58**
Blue-Capped Cordon Bleu **115**
Blue-Crowned Hanging Parrot **78**
Blue-Crowned Motmot **96**
Blue-Faced Parrot Finch **122**
Blue-Fronted Amazon Parrot **88**
Blue-Headed Pionus Parrot **86**
Blue-Headed Waxbill *see* Blue-Capped Cordon Bleu
Blue-Winged Parakeet **71**
Blue-Winged Siva **106**
Bobwhite 46, **48**
Bombay Avadavat 118
Bombycilla cedrorum (Cedar Waxwing) **101**
Border Canary *136*, 137
Bourke's Parakeet *56*, **70**
box cages 8, 9
Branta canadensis (Canada Goose) **22**
Branta ruficollis (Red-Breasted Goose) **22**
breeding 16–17, *16, 17*
breeding cages 9–11, *10*
broken limbs 149
Bronze Mannikin **124**
Brotogeris versicolurus (Canary-Winged Parakeet) **85**
Bubo bengalensis (Bengal Eagle Owl) **35**
Bubo bubo (European Eagle Owl) **34**
Bubo virginianus (Great Horned Owl) **35**
Bucephala clangula (European Goldeneye) **25**
budgerigars *13*, 56, 57, *57*, **72–5**
Bulbuls **100**

Bullfinch **129**
Bullfinches *16*, 113
buntings 110
Burrowing Owl **38**
Buteo buteo (European Buzzard) **31**
Buteo jamaicensis (Red-Tailed Hawk) **31**
buzzards 28, 29, **31**

C

Cacatua galerita (Greater Sulfur-Crested Cockatoo) **61**
Cacatua goffini (Goffin's Cockatoo) **62**
Cacatua moluccensis (Moluccan Cockatoo) **62**
cages 8, 9–10
    box cages 8, 9
    breeding cages 9–11, *10*
Cairina moschata (Muscovy Duck) **27**
California Quail 46, *49*
Callipepla squamata (Scaled Quail) **49**
Canada Goose *18–19, 21*, **22**
canaries 9, 10, 11, 12, *13*, 14, 110, **134–7**
    aviaries 137
    breeding 137
    exhibiting 137
    feather problems 151
    feeding 137
Canary-Winged Parakeet **85**
Cape Dove *see* Namaqua Dove
Capsychus malabaricus (White-Rumped Shama) **103**
carduline finches 110
Carduelis chloris (Greenfinch) **127**
Carduelis spinus (Siskin) **127**
Carolina Duck 23
Cassyphla niveicapilla (Snow-Headed Robin Chat) **102**
Cedar Waxwing **101**
Celestial Parrotlet **85**
Chaffinch **126**
Chalcophaps indica (Emerald Dove) **44**
Chattering Lory **60**
Cherry Finch **123**
Chestnut-Eared Finch *see* Zebra Finch
Chinese Painted Quail 17, 46, *47*, 48
Chloebia gouldiae (Gouldian Finch) **122**
Chloropsis aurifrons (Golden-Fronted Fruitsucker) **99**
Chrysolophus pictus (Golden Pheasant) **53**
Cinnyricinclus leucogaster (Amethyst Starling) **140**
CITES 92, 110
clematis 12, *12*
close ringing 28, 92
Coccothraustes coccothraustes (Hawfinch) **128**

Cockatiel 56, **63**
cockatoos 56, **60–62**
Colinus virginianus (Bobwhite) 48
Colius indicus (Red-Faced Mousebird) **94**
Columba livia (Rock Dove) 40, 45
Combassou **132**
Common Cordon Bleu 115
Common Firefinch **115**
Common Grenadier Waxbill *see* Violet-Eared Waxbill
Common Mynah *138*, **143**
Common Peafowl **55**
Common Pheasant 46
Common Starling **142**
Common Waxbill *see* St. Helena Waxbill
conures 56, **83**, **84**
Corvus corax (Raven) **147**
Corvus monedula (Jackdaw) **146**
Cosmopsarus regius (Royal Starling) **141**
Coturnix coromandelica (Rain Quail) **50**
Coturnix japonica (Japanese Quail) **48**
Crested Norwich Canary 137
Crested Pigeon *40*
Crimson Finch 130
Crossoptilon crossoptilon (White Eared Pheasant) 52
Cut-Throat Finch **125**
Cyanocorax yncas (Green Jay) **145**
Cyanoptila cyanomelaena (Japanese Blue Flycatcher) **107**
Cyanoramphus novaezelandiae (Red-Fronted Kakariki) **68**

D

Dacelo novaeguineae (Kookaburra) **95**
dehydration 149
Deroptyus accipitrinus (Hawk-Headed Parrot) **89**
Desmarest's Fig Parrot **64**
Diamond Dove **41**
Diamond Sparrow (Diamond Firetail) *113*, **119**
disease, dealing with 148–51
  dehydration 149
  feather problems 151
  home treatment materials 148, *148*
  injuries 149
  parasites 151
  preventive medicines 150
  probiotic additives 150
  quarantine 148, 150
  zoonoses 150
  see also individual diseases
DNA testing 16–17, 80, 92
Dominant Pied Blue Budgerigar *75*
double breeding cages 10
Double Yellow-Headed Amazon **89**
double-clutching 17
doves 40, **41–4**, 45
ducks and geese **22–27**
  breeding 21
  pinioning 21
  protection from predators 21

and water 20–21
  wing clipping 21
Dunnock **101**
Dusky Lory **59**
Dutch Canary 137
Dwarf Fig Parrot **64**

E

Eclectus r. rotatus (Grand Eclectus Parrot) **65**
ectoparasites 151
egg lethargy 149
egg pulling 17
Emblema guttata (Diamond Sparrow) **119**
Emerald Dove **44**
endoparasites 151
English Call Duck **25**
English Fallow Budgerigar *74*
enteritis 150, *150*
Eolophus roseicapillus (Rose-Breasted Cockatoo) **61**
Eos bornea (Red Lory) **58**
Eos reticulata (Blue Streaked Lory) **58**
Erithacus calliope (Siberian Rubythroat) **102**
Erythrura trichroa (Blue-Faced Parrot Finch) **122**
Estrilda astrild (St. Helena Waxbill) **117**
Estrilda caerulescens (Lavender Finch) **116**
Estrilda melpoda (Orange-Cheeked Waxbill) **117**
Eubucco bourcierii (Red-Headed Barbet) **97**
Euplectes afer (Yellow Bishop) **133**
European Blackbird **104**
European Buzzard **31**
European Eagle Owl **34**
European Goldeneye **25**
European Jay **144**, **145**
European Kestrel 32
European Starling **138**
European Wigeon **23**
Excalfactoria chinensis (Chinese Painted Quail) **47**

F

Fairy Bluebird **100**
Falco peregrinus (Peregrine Falcon) **33**
Falco sparverius (American Kestrel) **32**
falconry 28
falcons 8, **28–9**, **33**
feather problems 151
feather-plucking 17, 137, *150*, 151
feeding **14–15**, *15*
Fig Parrots **64**
finches 10, 11, 12, 110–13, **116**, **120–23**, **125–9**
Fischer's Whydah **132**
flukes 151
Forpus coelestis (Celestial Parrotlet) **85**
fowl pest 148
Fringilla coelebs (Chaffinch) **126**
fruit 14, 92

G

Galah *see* Rose-Breasted Cockatoo
Gallicolumba luzonica (Luzon Bleeding-Heart Pigeon) **44**
Garden Fantail **45**
Garrulus glandarius (European Jay) **144**
Garrulax albogularis (White-Crested Laughing Thrush) **105**
geese, ducks and **20–27**
Geopelia cuneata (Diamond Dove) **41**
Geopelia striata (Zebra Dove) **41**
German Roller Canary 134, 137
Gloster Canary 134, *136*, 151
Goffin's Cockatoo **62**
Golden Pheasant 46, **53**
Golden Song Sparrow **133**
Golden-Breasted Waxbill **119**
Golden-Fronted Fruitsucker **99**
Golden-Headed Fig Parrot **64**
Golden-Mantled Rosella **67**
goldfinches 111
Goldie's Lorikeet *2–3*, **59**
Goliath Cockatoo **60**
Goshawks 148
Gouldian Finch *111*, **122**
Gracula r. religiosa (Greater Hill Mynah) **144**
Grand Eclectus Parrot **65**
Grass Parakeets 56
Great Gray Owl **38**
Great Horned Owl **35**
Greater Hill Mynah **144**
Greater Sulfur-Crested Cockatoo 56, **61**
green food 14
Green Jay **145**
Green-Winged Macaw **81**
Green-Winged Pytilia **114**
Greenfinch 111, **127**

H

Hahn's Macaw **83**
Harris Hawk *28*, **32**
Hartlaub's Touraco **94**
Hawfinch **128**
Hawk-Headed Parrot **89**
hawks 17, *28*, *29*, **30**, **31**, **32**
heating 11, *11*
Heck's Grass Finch **120**
Himalayan Monal Pheasant **51**
honeysuckle 12, *12*
Hyacinth Macaw 56
Hypargos niveoguttatus (Peter's Twinspot) **114**

I

Indian Hill Mynah 138
Indian Peafowl 46
Indian Ring-Necked Parakeet **79**
Indian Silverbill 123
Indian Zosterop 90, **109**
Indigo Bird *see* Combassou
insectivores 15
Irena puella (Fairy Bluebird) **100**

J

Jackdaw **146**
Japanese Blue Flycatcher **107**
Japanese Quail 17, 46, **48**
Java Sparrow **125**
jays 138, **144**, **145**

K

Kakarikis 56, **68**
Kestrels 32
Kookaburra 90, *93*, **95**

L

laburnum 12, *12*
Lacewing Yellow Budgerigar 72
Lady Amherst's Pheasant 53
Lagonosticta senegala (Common
    Firefinch) **115**
Lamprotornis caudatus (Long-Tailed
    Glossy Starling) **139**
Lancashire Canary 134
Lancashire Coppy Canary 137
Laughing Dove *see* Senegal Dove
Lavender Finch **116**
Laysan Teal **24**
Lear's Macaw 16
Leiothrix argentauris (Silver-Eared
    Mesia) **105**
Leothrix lutea (Pekin Robin) **106**
Lesser Sulfur-Crested Cockatoo 61
Lettered Aracari **98**
Leucopsar rothschild (Rothschild's
    Starling) **143**
licensing 28, 90
lighting 11
Linnet **128**
Little Owl **36**
Lonchura cantans (African Silverbill) **123**
Lonchura culcullata (Bronze Mannikin)
    124
Lonchura striata (White-Backed
    Mannikin) **124**
Long-Eared Owl **39**
Long-Tailed Glossy Starling **139**
Long-Tailed Grass Finch **120**
Lophophorus impeyanus (Himalayan
    Monal Pheasant) **51**
Lophortyx californica (California Quail)
    49
Lophura diardi (Siamese Fireback
    Pheasant) **52**
Lophura nycthemera (Silver Pheasant) **54**
Loriculus galgulus (Blue-Crowned
    Hanging Parrot) **78**
lories 56, **58–60**
lorikeets 56, **59**
Lorius garrulus (Chattering Lory) **60**
Luzon Bleeding-Heart Pigeon **44**

M

macaws 9, *13*, 56, **80–83**
magpies 138, **145**, **146**
Malachite Sunbird **109**
Mandarin Duck *18–19*, *20*, **23**
Mannikins **124**

Masked Dove *see* Namaqua Dove
Masked Grass Finch 120
Melba Finch (Green-Winged Pytilia)
    114, **131**
Melopsittacus undulatus (Budgerigar) **73**
Military Macaw **82**
Minia cyanouroptera (Blue-Winged
    Siva) **106**
Moluccan Cocktaoo **62**
Momotus momota (Blue-Crowned
    Motmot) **96**
Monk Parakeet *see* Quaker Parakeet
Motmots **96**
Muscovy Duck **27**
Myiopsitta monachus (Quaker Parakeet)
    84
mynahs 138, *138*, **143**, **144**

N

Namaqua Dove **43**
Napoleon Weaver *see* Yellow Bishop
Nectarinia famosa (Malachite Sunbird)
    109
Nectarinia senegalensis (Scarlet-Chested
    Sunbird) **108**
Neochima phaeton (Crimson Finch) **120**
Neochima ruficauda (Star Finch) **120**
Neophema bourkii (Bourke's Parakeet) **70**
Neophema chrysostoma (Blue-Winged
    Parakeet) **71**
Neophema pulchella (Turquoise Grass
    Parakeet) **71**
Neophema splendida (Splendid Parakeet)
    69
nesting boxes *13*
Newcastle disease (fowl pest) 148, *150*
Niltava sundara (Rufous-Bellied
    Niltava) **108**
Norwich Canary *134*, 151
Nyctea scandiaca (Snowy Owl) **39**
Nymphicus hollandicus (Cockatiel) **63**

O

Oena capensis (Namaqua Dove) **43**
Opopsitta diophthalma (Dwarf Fig
    Parrot) **64**
Orange-Breasted Waxbill **119**
Orange-Cheeked Waxbill **117**
Orange-Winged Parrot **88**
Otus scops (Scops Owl) **37**
owls 28, 29, **34–9**

P

Padda oryzivora (Java Sparrow) **125**
Paddy Bird *see* Java Sparrow
Palm Cockatoo **60**
Parabuteo unicinctus (Harris Hawk) **32**
Paradise Whydah 114, **131**
parakeets 11, 12, *13*, 14, 56, *56*, **66–71**,
    78, 84, 85
parasites 151
Parisian Frill Canary 137, *137*
parrots 8, 9, 11, 14, 16, 17, **58–89**
    aviaries 57
    breeding 56, 57

diseases 148, 151
    feeding 56–7
partridge **50**
Pavo cristatus (Common Peafowl) **55**
Peach-Faced Lovebird **77**
Peafowl **55**
Pekin Robin 90, 93, **106**
Peregrine Falcon 33, 150
Peter's Twinspot (Peter's Firefinch)
    114
pheasants 14, 17, 46, *46*, **51–4**
Philippine Glossy Starling **139**
Phoenicurus leucocephalus (White-
    Capped Redstart) **103**
Pica pica (Magpie) **146**
pigeons 40, *40*, **44**, **45**, 148
Pin-Tailed Whydah 117, **130**, 131
Pionites melanocephala (Black-Headed
    Caique) **86**
Pionus menstruus (Blue-Headed Pionus
    Parrot) **86**
plants 12, *12*, 92–3, 137, 154–5
Platycercus eximius celiciae (Golden-
    Mantled Rosella) **67**
Plum-Headed Finch *see* Cherry Finch
Poephila acuticauda (Long-Tailed Grass
    Finch) **120**
Poephila guttata (Zebra Finch) **121**
Poicephalus senegalus (Senegal Parrot) **77**
poisons 11–12, *12*
Polytelis alexandrae (Princess of Wales
    Parakeet) **67**
Polytelis swainsonii (Barraband Parakeet)
    66
ponds 13, 20
predators 21
Princess of Wales Parakeet **67**
probiotic additives 150
Probosciger aterrimus (Palm Cockatoo)
    60
Prunela modularis (Dunnock) **101**
Psephotus haematonotus (Red-Rumped
    Parakeet) **68**
pseudotuberculosis 150
psittacine beak and feather disease 151
psittacosis (PBFD) 150, *151*
Psittacula eupatria (Alexandrine
    Parakeet) **78**
Psittacula krameri manillensis (Indian
    Ring-Necked Parakeet) **79**
Psittaculirostris desmarestii (Desmarest's
    Fig Parrot) **64**
Psittacus erithacus (African Grey Parrot)
    76
Pteroglossus inscriptus (Lettered Aracari)
    98
Purple Grenadier **132**
Pycnonotus jocosus (Red-Whiskered
    Bulbul) **100**
Pyrrhula pyrrhula (Bullfinch) **129**
Pyrrhura frontalis (Red-Bellied Conure)
    84
Pytilia melba (Green-Winged Pytilia)
    114

Q

quail 17, 46, **47–50**
Quaker Parakeet **84**
quarantine 148, 150

R

Rain Quail **50**
Ramphastros toco (Toco Toucan) **98**
Raven **147**
Red Avadavat **118**
Red Lory **58**
red mites 151
Red-Bellied Conure **84**
Red-Bellied Macaw **82**
Red-Billed Blue Magpie **145**
Red-Billed Firefinch (Common
    Firefinch) **115**, 132
Red-Billed Hornbill **97**
Red-Billed Weaver 111
Red-Breasted Goose **22**
Red-Cheeked Cordon Bleu 115
Red-Eared Waxbill **117**
Red-Eyed Lutino *73*
Red-Faced Mousebird **94**
Red-Factor Canary *134*
Red-Fronted Kakariki **68**
Red-Headed Barnet **97**
Red-Rumped Parakeet **68**
Red-Tailed Hawk *4–5*, *29*, **31**
Red-Whiskered Bulbul **100**
Red-Winged Pytilia **114**
redpolls 111, 113
Reeves Pheasant *46*, **53**
Ribbon Finch *see* Cut-Throat Finch
Ring Dove **40**
Rock Dove **40**, 45
rodents 11–12, 13
Roller Canaries 134, 137, 148
Rollulus roulroul (Roulroul Partridge) **50**
Rose-Breasted Cockatoo **61**
Roseate *see* Rose-Breasted Cockatoo
Rothschild's Mynah **138**
Rothschild's Starling **143**
Roulroul Partridge **50**
Royal Starling **141**
Rufous-Bellied Niltava **108**
Russian vine 12, 93

S

St. Helena Waxbill 113, **117**
salmonella food poisoning 150
Scaled Quail **49**
scaly face *151*
Scarlet Macaw *4*, **81**
Scarlet Tanager 93
Scarlet-Chested Sunbird 90, **108**
Scops Owl **37**
Scotch Fancy Canary **137**
Screech Owl *see* Barn Owl
seed eaters, small 11, 110–13, **114–34**
    breeding 111, 113
    feeding 111–13
    groups 110
    housing 112–13
    law 111

Senegal Dove **42**
Senegal Parrot **77**
Serinus canaria **134**
Siamese Fireback Pheasant **52**
Siberian Rubythroat **102**
Silver Pheasant 46, **54**
Silver-Eared Mesia **105**
single-species collections 6
Siskin *110*, *112*, 113, **127**
small seed eaters *see* seed eaters, small
small softbills *see* softbills, small
Snow-Headed Robin Chat **102**
soaked seed 14, 112
Society Finch *see* Bengalese Mannikin
softbills, small 11, **94–109**
    breeding 90, 92, 93
    feeding 92
    proof of captive breeding 90, 92
Southern Grackle **144**
Spangled Cobalt Budgerigar *72*
Spanish Timbrados Canary **137**
Sparrowhawk (UK) *30*, 32
Sparrowhawk (US) 32
sparrows 110, *113*, **119**, **125**, **133**
Spix's Macaw **56**
Splendid Parakeet **69**
Spreo Starling **140**
Spreo superbus (Spreo Starling) **140**
Stafford Canary 134, *136*
Star Finch **120**
starlings **138–47**
Steel Finch *see* Combassou
Straw-Tailed Whydah *see* Fischer's
    Whydah
Strawberry Finch **118**
Streptopelia senegalensis (Senegal Dove)
    42
Strix aluco (Tawny Owl) **37**
Strix nebulosa (Great Gray Owl) **38**
Sturnus vulgaris (Common Starling)
    142
Sulfur-Crested Cockatoos **61**
Sun Conure **83**
Sunbirds 90, **108**, **109**
Superb Starling *see* Spreo Starling
symbols guide 7
Syrmaticus reevesii (Reeves Pheasant)
    53

T

Tambourine Dove **42**
Tauraco hartlaub (Hartlaub's Touraco)
    94
Tauraco leucotis (White-Cheeked
    Touraco) **95**
Tawny Owl **37**
temperature control 11
ticks *151*
Tiger Finch **118**
Timneh Grey Parrot **76**
Tockus erythrorhynchus (Red-Billed
    Hornbill) **97**
Toco Toucan 90, *91*, **98**
Toucans 90, *91*, **98**
Touracos **94**, **95**

treble breeding cages 9–10, *10*
Trichoglossus goldiei (Goldie's Lorikeet)
    59
Tufted Duck **24**
Turdus merula (European Blackbird)
    104
Turquoise Grass Parakeet **71**
Turtur tympanistria (Tambourine Dove)
    42
Tyto alba (Barn Owl) **36**

U

Uraeginthus cyanocephala (Blue-Capped
    Cordon Bleu) **115**
Uraeginthus grantina (Violet-Eared
    Waxbill) **116**
Urocissa erythrorhyncha (Red-Billed
    Blue Magpie) **145**

V

ventilation 11
vermin 11–12, 14
Vidua chalbeata (Combassou) **132**
Vidua fischeri (Fischer's Whydah) **132**
Vidua macroura (Pin-Tailed Whydah)
    117, **130**
Vidua paradisaea (Paradise Whydah)
    131
Violet Starling *see* Amethyst Starling
Violet-Eared Waxbill **116**

W

waterfowl 13, 14
waxbills 16, 110, 111, 112–13, **116–19**
weavers 110, 111, **133**
White Eared Pheasant **52**
White Owl *see* Barn Owl
White-Backed Mannikin **124**
White-Capped Redstart **103**
White-Cheeked Touraco **95**
White-Crested Duck **26**
White-Crested Laughing Thrush **105**
White-Fronted Amazon Parrot **87**
White-Naped Yuhina **107**
White-Rumped Shama **103**
whydahs 114, 117, **130**, 131, **131**, **132**
wing clipping 21
Wood Pigeon **40**
worms 151

Y

Yellow Bishop **133**
Yellow-Headed Amazons **89**
Yellow-Winged Green Budgerigar *72*
yew 12
Yorkshire Canary **134**
Yuhina bakeri (White-Naped Yuhina)
    107

Z

Zebra Dove **41**
Zebra Finch **121**
zoonoses 150
Zosterops palpebrosa (Indian Zosterop)
    109

Credits

Key: a above, b below, l left, r right, c center

Aquila: 16b (Roger Thomas), 26a, 27a, 45c (Mike Wilkes), 57 (M. Gilroy), 111 (M. Gilroy), 113, 128a

Ardea London Ltd: 2, 18 (J.A. Bailey), 22a (Kenneth Fink), 22b (J.A. Bailey), 23a (J.A. Bailey), 23b (Ian Beames), 24a (Kenneth Fink), 24b (J.A. Bailey), 25 (John Daniels), 28 (Kenneth Fink), 30 (R.T. Smith), 31 (R.T. Smith), 31a (R.J.C. Blewitt), 31b (Gregory K. Scott), 32a (Francois Gohier), 32b (Kenneth Fink), 33 (Piers Cavendish), 34 (Stefen Myers), 35a (Kenneth Fink), 35b (Peter Steyn), 36a & b (Ian Beames), 37a (John Daniels), 37b (Z. Tunka), 38a (John S. Dunning), 38b (Kenneth Fink), 39a (Wardene Weisser), 39b (D. Morris), 40 (Dennis Avon), 41a (Dennis Avon), 41b (Kenneth Fink), 42a & b (Dennis Avon), 43 (Dennis Avon), 44a & b (Kenneth Fink), 47 (Dennis Avon), 48b (Jack Swedburg), 49a (Dennis Avon), 49b (Kenneth Fink), 50a (Dennis Avon), 50b (Kenneth Fink), 51 (Joanna van Gruisen), 52a & b (Kenneth Fink), 53a (Kenneth Fink), 53b (Ian Beames), 54 (Kenneth Fink), 55 (Ake Lindau), 56 (Dennis Avon), 58a (Dennis Avon), 58b (Kenneth Fink), 59a & b (Dennis Avon), 60a (J.M. Labat), 60b (Kenneth Fink), 61a (Dennis Avon), 61b (J.M. Labat), 62a (Kenneth Fink), 62b (Dennis Avon), 63 (Dennis Avon), 64a (Kenneth Fink), 64b (J.P. Ferrero), 65 (Dennis Avon), 67a & b (Dennis Avon), 68a (Dennis Avon), 69 (Dennis Avon), 70 (Dennis Avon), 71a (John Mason), 71b (Dennis Avon), 76 (Kenneth Fink), 77a (John Daniels), 77b (Dennis Avon), 78a & b (Dennis Avon), 79 (Dennis Avon), 80 (Kenneth Fink), 81a (Francois Gohier), 81b (Wardene Weisser), 82a (Kenneth Fink), 82b (Dennis Avon), 83a & b (Dennis Avon), 84a (P. Morris), 84b (Ian Beames), 85a (Dennis Avon), 86a (Dennis Avon), 86b (P. Morris), 87 (Francois Gohier), 88 (Dennis Avon), 89a (Dennis Avon), 89b (Kenneth Fink), 94a (Alan Weaving), 94b (Kenneth Fink), 95a (Ian Beames), 95b (J.P. Ferrero), 96 (M.D. England), 97 (M.D. England), 97b (R.M. Bloomfield), 98a (Kenneth Fink), 98b (J.M. Labat), 99 (Dennis Avon), 100a & b (Dennis Avon), 101a (Dennis Avon), 101b (J.A. Bailey), 102a (Irene Neufeldt), 103a (Dennis Avon), 103b (M.D. England), 104 (D.W. Greenslade), 105a (Wardene Weisser), 105b (D.W. Greenslade), 106a & b (Dennis Avon), 107a & b (Dennis Avon), 108 (Dennis Avon), 109a (Peter Steyn), 109b (Dennis Avon), 114a (J.J. Brooks), 114b (Dennis Avon), 115a & b (Dennis Avon), 116a (Dennis Avon), 117a & b (Dennis Avon), 118 (Dennis Avon), 119a & b (Dennis Avon), 120a (Dennis Avon), 120b (F. Collet), 121a (Donald Molly), 121b (Trounson), 122a (M.D. England), 122b (Dennis Avon), 123a & b (Dennis Avon), 124a (J.A. Bailey), 124b (Dennis Avon), 125a (Dennis Avon), 126 (J.A. Bailey), 127a & b (Dennis Avon), 128b (Dennis Avon), 130 (Ferrero Labat), 131 (P. Morris), 132a & b (Dennis Avon), 133a (Dennis Avon), 133b (J.S. Wightman), 139b (P. Blasdale), 140a & b (Dennis Avon), 141 (Dennis Avon), 143a (Dennis Avon), 143 (G.K. Brown), 144a (Dennis Avon), 144b (R.J.C. Blewitt), 145a (Kenneth Fink), 145b (Dennis Avon), 146a & b (J.B. & S. Bottomley), 147 (P. Morris)

Dr. Alan Beaumont: 73, 91, 102b, 116b, 139

Tom Ennis: 4b

Mike Lane: 26b, 27b

Cyril Laubscher: 8, 17a & b, 72a & b, 74, 75, 134, 135, 136al, ar, & b, 137, 150bl, bcl, & bcr, 151bl, bcl, & br

Harry Smith Horticultural Collection: 12a, b, & r

Oxford Scientific Films: 66 (Steve Turner), 68b (Tony Tilford)

Tom J. Ulrich: 85b

Graham Wellstead: 29b

Windrush: 4a, 20 (Les Borg), 21 (A.&E. Morris), 46, 48a (David Tipling), 90 (Peter Basterfield), 93, 110 (John Hollis), 112 (Richard Revels), 125b, 129, 138, 142 (Richard Revels)

The birds shown in the following uncaptioned photographs can be identified as follows: pages 2–3 Goldie's Lorikeet; page 4: Scarlet Macaw; pages 4–5 Red-Tailed Hawk; pages 18–19 Mandarin Ducks